SM06002465
? /07
.95
(Buc)

KT-485-846

Myths, Risks and Sexuality

Edited by

Karen Buckley and Paul Head

Russell House Publishing

ST MARTIN'S COLLEGE
LANCASTER LIBRARY

First published in 2000 by:
Russell House Publishing Ltd
4 St George's House
Uplyme Road
Lyme Regis
Dorset DT7 3LS

Tel: 01297 443948
Fax: 01297 442722
e-mail: help@russellhouse.co.uk

© Karen Buckley and Paul Head and the various contributors

All rights reserved. No part of this publication may be reproduced,
stored in a retrieval system or transmitted in any form, or by any means,
electronic, mechanical, photocopying, recording or otherwise,
without the prior permission of the copyright holder and the publisher.

British Library Cataloguing-in-publication Data:
A catalogue record for this book is available from the British Library.

ISBN: 1-898924-36-8

Typeset by TW Typesetting, Plymouth, Devon

Printed by Hobbs, Totton, Southampton

Russell House Publishing
is a group of social work, probation, education
and youth and community work practitioners
and academics working in collaboration with a
professional publishing team.
Our aim is to work closely with the field to
produce innovative and valuable materials to
help managers, trainers, practitioners and
students.
We are keen to receive feedback on
publications and new ideas for future projects.

Contents

Preface

Asking Questions and Getting Heard

Michelle Meloy's chapter ends with the remark 'I wish someone would ask the question'. That rather describes the motivations that lead to this book. As editors we wished just that, or rather that they would ask the right questions. Questions that might get them some useful answers.

In our main employment we both worked constantly with the most unattractive facets of human behaviour, i.e. the capacity to be violent and abusive to the vulnerable. We were constantly being asked to share in judgements as to a person's potential for repeating such behaviour. We were also being asked to share in developing policies and courses designed to minimise such possibilities.

We also spend time as trainers, running courses on understanding sexuality and the discrimination that surrounds it. This time we found ourselves trying to demystify judgements about risk and dangerousness. Often it was like being faced with a mirror image. On the one hand we met a world where colleagues didn't always want to acknowledge the existence of domestic violence and child abuse, on the other we found ourselves dealing with a deliberate demonising of certain groups in society. Why weren't the right questions being asked on both counts?

Equally, we found that sometimes those who did ask uncomfortable questions were marginalised. Devalue the messenger, as it were, and you can obliterate the message.

Sometimes the process of what happened to those who asked difficult questions about practice was akin to what occurs when so-called minorities raise their issues; polite, or not so polite, silence.

We therefore collected together a group of colleagues who do ask questions and who often are unheard. There is some interesting practice out there and we wanted to get it publicised. If this initially seems an odd collection of essays we hope that by the end the reader will see connections without the need for our explanations. Those connections are about refusing to allow your judgement to be compromised by stereotypes, around sexuality, and thus making some uncompromising and uncomfortable points across a range of topic areas.

A Personal Note

We would accordingly like to pay tribute to our contributors, some of whom have not written for publication before, and who have busy personal and professional lives. Some of them have rather plaintively told us they did not know what they were letting themselves in for. We would like to thank Russell House for not being fazed by this, and for their encouragement. Finally as individuals, we would like to thank Di Bevan and Richard Green for endless tolerance and support.

About the Authors

Clarence Allen works as a community worker with young people. He is also an experienced trainer, drawing on his life experience as a black gay man.

Karen Buckley is a senior probation officer, currently working in a prison setting, who also teaches and publishes on sexuality, gender and masculinity.

Jan Clare is a lecturer in social work at the University of Central England and a senior probation officer with West Midlands. She also provides training for external agencies on sexuality.

Paul Head is a former probation officer and youth worker. Until recently he was working as a specialist group worker and acting as one of the convenors of 'Lesbians and Gays in Probation'. He is now a senior forensic social worker in a special hospital.

Victoria Hodgett is a senior probation officer who has an established track record in groupwork with sex offenders. Until very recently Victoria worked as a group worker in a prison specialising in sex offender work. She now manages a unit for sex offenders who are considered too dangerous to be released to the community.

Maggie Metcalfe is a probation officer who has a long-term commitment to working with dangerous women. She formerly spent six years running a day facility for women, and has also worked with male perpetrators of sexual and other violence.

Michelle Meloy was for several years a probation officer in Chicago, U.S.A. and is now a research assistant at the University of Delaware.

Ted Perry is a probation officer who previously worked in a prison setting with sex offenders. He is a trainer on child protection, and also publishes and teaches on masculinity and work with sex offenders.

David Phillips, a former teacher, is now a probation officer. David was for some years a group worker with sexual and other violent offenders and is now a practice teacher.

Jo Thompson is a senior probation officer with a particular interest in sex offender work. Jo is a former co-chair of The National Association of Probation Officers.

Graeme Vaughan is a probation officer in Norfolk who is currently working on risk assessment.

Leonie Williams is a former probation officer and trainer on domestic violence, who now works with the families of drug abusers.

CHAPTER 1

Stereotypes Can be Dangerous: Working with Sexuality, Power and Risk

Karen Buckley and Paul Head

Sniggering about sexuality, unfortunate or oppressive jokes and embarrassed laughter are all so commonplace. More rarely do we encounter talking about 'sex': or rather, talking about sex openly, honestly and comfortably. Some people take the line that sex is 'private' and should not be talked about at all. Most people have firm positions on popular subjects including under-age sex or pornography; the reaction to such subjects being hot-headed debate, often mixed with embarrassed silence.

What is less obvious is the way that sexuality is used in such discussions. Whilst many of us have had our best and most uplifting experiences through the exercise of our sexuality, equally, some have had their most profoundly abusive and damaging experiences in the sexual arena. Some of this is through openly abusive and violent behaviour. Some originates in being denied access to positive affirmation of sexual identity, or being persistently and unpleasantly sexualised.

Where people can be defined by their sexual activity and are deemed to be breaking the rules of appropriate behaviour, they are usually the butts of humour or their differences are ignored. Either situation diminishes them and, perhaps more importantly, their humanity. One cannot avoid the conclusion that attitudes to sexuality are constructed with the potential for 'abuse of power' as a central function. Our contention, as editors, is that these attitudes are deliberately fostered. The result is to prevent real discussion of what constitutes abusive behaviour and, as a consequence, provides easy scapegoats.

This book has come together around the theme of talking about this hidden world. We are trying to examine the role of sexuality openly and learn. Some of the contributors are academics and teachers and write as such, some are practitioners, some reflect on personal experience. All are trying to generate debate, because they have found it impossible to work to their personal and professional satisfaction under the confines of 'popular' or stereotypical thinking. The work is intended to be accessible and relatively jargon free. It is intended for anyone who asks for an understanding about the person they are working with. It challenges the ideas prevalent in heterosexist assumptions. It dares to make clear the way attraction and, in

1

particular, sexual attraction influences decision-making. Whether they ask it about themselves, their work or the behaviour of others.

The Contributors

As editors, we have drawn together a collection of practitioner experiences around a single theme or message. Our concern is that we will never produce more than piecemeal adjustments to the problems that human behaviour presents, until we stop perceiving such behaviour stereotypically. What connects our contributors, across race, gender, sexuality and agency divides, as well as in one case several thousands of miles, is a commitment to clarity of thought rather than acceptance of 'the way it is'. Sometimes, this commitment has come from personal experience; Clarence Allen's thinking, for example, has been informed by his life experience as a black gay man in a racist and homophobic environment.

For some, years of practice have developed an understanding, a consciousness. Ted Perry and Michelle Meloy have been working as probation officers on either side of the Atlantic, both specialising in sex offender work, and have come to very similar conclusions about the changes needed to stereotypical thinking if they are to challenge, effectively, perpetrators' behaviour towards their victims. These are similar to the conclusions that Jo Thompson and Victoria Hodgett arrive at.

Sometimes, the concern that provoked the thinking behind the chapter has come from lack of knowledge, a sudden discovery that the world is not constructed as life experience and professional activity has prepared one for. Leonie Williams and David Phillips, for example, began working together, sharing what they knew in an attempt to learn about and support transgender people who happened to also be criminals. The chapters by Graeme Vaughan and Maggie Metcalfe are an attempt to take forward practice in an area where they have felt that traditional methods of risk assessment were less than effective because of stereotypical thinking. In the penultimate chapter Jan Clare offers ideas about how training might open minds to the issues.

The theme of honest evaluation of stereotypes which runs through the book has linked work that colleagues in probation services have undertaken with criminals, with work of colleagues in other agencies in providing advice and support to people suffering disadvantage and discrimination. It links training activity, in relation to thinking on the issue of equal opportunities, with the provision of effective challenge to inappropriate behaviour. One of the issues motivating us is that such work has often been undertaken compartmentally. Thus, this book attempts to link a range of topic areas and connect learning. From the area of thinking about equalities and empowerment we have taken the learning around sexuality and gender; this has then been blended with learning that has arisen from work with those who behave oppressively and criminally.

An important concept in this context has been that of cognitive distortion or reframing the world to fit with one's own needs and desires. For example, from work with sex offenders we understand that someone who has raped will 'explain' the situation in ways that make this behaviour acceptable at least to themselves. This kind of distorted thinking process is very familiar to anyone from a minority group. It explains the way they have been described. Any black person, for example, knows that black people are as varied culturally and behaviourally as any other randomly selected group but often they have had their behaviour interpreted using white stereotypes and white cognitive distortions.

This book sets out to make connections for anyone who has concerns about this process, who wants to challenge it or who just wants to find out how others deal with it. It will hopefully be accessible not just to those who work with stereotyping but also those who feel its impact and are irritated by it.

The Continuum of Behaviour

Much human behaviour, we would suggest, lies on a continuum; a spectrum. Many of the worst acts perpetuated by human beings on each other can be viewed as extensions of popular cultural myths, fantasies or beliefs. Men who beat their partners are offered legal challenge or counselling, this may neglect the fact that the couple live in the context of a society that bombards men with images of passive women or women as objects of men's desire. The man's logic may tell him that society is duplicitous which may increase his anger. How do you, in fact, access the man's 'logic' to work with him, without being corrupted by it? As a worker you will have had precisely the same cultural experiences which will have impacted on you.

We are confronted *too*, when teaching or counselling or working with offenders, with a sense of disbelief. This results in a refusal to contemplate the extent of human behaviour or to change thinking patterns on the part of colleagues, as well as offenders. The refusal to acknowledge and respect gay identity, we encounter when training professional workers on sexuality, is paralleled by refusal of the same workers to see the extent of abusive behaviours perpetrated by 'ordinary' people. It is as if the bulk of society prefers to think simplistically, along pre-arranged patterns, for such thinking gives an illusion of safety.

It is such thinking that permeates the institutional processes of our society. Workers in child protection face as much opprobrium if they outline a problem, which cannot be proved (as in the Cleveland Enquiry), as when they fail to protect a vulnerable child (as in the Beckford Enquiry). One could be forgiven for making the assumption that the general public and major institutions largely want things swept under the carpet.

What became clear to us, and has perhaps occasioned the particular collection of contributions we have put together, is that there is a commonality of themes across many areas of work, when considering human sexual behaviour. The very fact that the areas are often compartmentalised avoids their full and open deconstruction.

All of our contributors were chosen because they are observing and/or working with an area of dangerous, risky and sensitive human behaviour; what people do in their most intimate contacts with each other and how this is reflected, used and abused in cultural images. For example, as Maggie Metcalfe illustrates, working with a woman offender involves more than just working with the woman and her behaviour. It involves working with society's images of dangerous women as they have impacted on the woman in court. The woman may have a better or worse deal than a man in similar circumstances, but she will have a different one. Equally, as Leonie Williams and David Phillips comment, no one relates to transgender people in a simple fashion. Contact with them is always tinged with our feelings and instincts about transsexuality. It is displayed in our failure to recognise the difference between transgender and transvestite, for example, and then to register that sexuality and gender have a distinctly separate and individual part to play in self definition.

Exploring the abusive behaviour of others reflects one's own behaviour like a mirror, the instinct is to deny the similarities. It is so much more comfortable to see oneself as a victim of the bad behaviour of others, because this allows one to distance oneself from responsibility of membership of the society that perpetrates it. To honestly contemplate one's own investment in society means accepting that one may be oppressive to some others. All our contributors have refused to participate in this process and have a determination, if necessary, to be a lone voice examining their own behaviours and attitudes, sometimes painfully, as they help others examine themselves and understand responsibility for their behaviour. Connecting these voices and themes, we believe, makes a powerful statement.

The Legal Framework

One difficulty workers and others encounter is that the problems of oppressive behaviour are sometimes enshrined in law. The legal framework of our society can be viewed as being aimed at controlling behaviour that is threatening to the status quo and to public attitudes, rather than focusing directly on the management and challenge of those who perpetrate abusive behaviours. There are a range of examples; the whole history of campaigns against domestic violence providing a rich seam of evidence (see, for example, Dobash and Dobash, 1992).

Equally, we have laws about restraining the behaviour of prostitutes but only recently has attention been paid to kerb crawlers. The consensual behaviour of gay men is policed in a way that criminalises many in situations where behaviour by heterosexual men is not viewed as illegal. Transgender people can, if they are lucky, access extensive counselling and surgery, but cannot yet formalise this process in a legal identity and change their birth certificate or legally marry. Interestingly, as a result of this, when a male to female transsexual is attracted to females and chooses to be in a lesbian relationship, she can then marry, as her birth certificate classifies her as a male.

Legal status is often translated into ceremonial oppression using the legal process and public denunciation to ensure self-censorship. Hence the problems faced by those whose sexuality is different, though consensual, who can be ashamed to acknowledge their difference, even to themselves. The law acts to prevent the confirmation of relationships and provides no public display of same-sex love.

The law, as it exists, also fails to protect in situations of any subtlety. Women and children who have been abused still have to effectively run away to be safe and there remains an in-built assumption that they may lie. 'Domestic' violence does not attract anything like the same penalties as stranger or street violence does and enforcement is still hinged with assumptions that the victim may have deserved or provoked the violence. There remains more power and willingness to remove victims than perpetrators. The chapter on the use of violence in same-sex relationships will also look at how oppression can produce a failure to identify a problem, or even to perceive it as being of equal value. Both this chapter and the chapter on black issues will look at the impact of self-censorship and the imposition of definitions of appropriate behaviours by others.

At the same time, one can identify in society a desire to find simple, quick fix, hide-it-away solutions, rather than tease out the implications of who is vulnerable, and who is abused, as the chapter by Ted Perry will outline. His detailing of the road to be travelled is indicative of the complexities of the topic. The vigilantes pursuing sex offenders in the community do not have complex solutions; they merely wish the problem to go away. They certainly do not want to contemplate any abusive content in their own behaviour or any sense of a continuum of human behaviours. Solutions such as registers of offenders are attractive and necessary but they are only about identifying the problem and can create an illusion of security and distance where in reality, there is none.

Defining the Territory

Any work of this kind has to start with the question: why is it like this? Why as a society are we so comfortable with a framework for monitoring behaviour which is slipshod and evasive? Why are we comfortable with scenarios which make working with sexuality so stressful and so incomplete in its challenges? Why do we fail so often to acknowledge complexity?

Afro-centric theorists have redefined and offered us the notion of dichotomous thinking. (Hill Collins, 1991). White European/North American thinking, they would suggest, is based on this notion which suggests that I can only visualise myself if I am different to or in opposition to you. I can only be good if I can see bad in another. Our gender roles, this theory would argue, are perceived as oppositional concepts. This has resonance when we contemplate the ways in which we as sexual beings are all taught to adhere to these roles. Often we are satirised as trying to ape the behaviour of the other gender, and thus compartmentalised, defined by heterosexist definitions of appropriate gendered behaviour. The problem that ensues from this is that the prevailing power group, in this context men, (but in other contexts white men and women or heterosexual men and women) can define themselves as in possession of the 'prized' or 'positive' qualities; and then use this to reinforce oppression and denial of rights to the other group.

Sexuality and our understanding of it is closely related to our perceptions of gender. Individuals learn gender appropriate sexual behaviours and, as the chapter on black issues demonstrates, there are variations in how the sexuality of black and white people is perceived, to the disadvantage of, and for the control of, black groups. Sexual stereotyping is used in the process of defining 'the others' when women, black people or gays are seen as responsible for being sexually provocative, or sexually predatory. In fact it can seem that those who are about to be dispossessed, are first made sexually responsible. In relation to attitudes to prostitution it has been suggested that, ' a history of sexual activity is used to differentiate different kinds of women' and that this is evidence of a 'relationship between a person's social identity and their sexual behaviour' (Srage, 1997, p139). These comments were made about prostitution, but the observations would also apply where sexuality is an ascribed rather than an evident factor in a situation.

Sexual and gendered behaviours are taught in confused and interconnected ways, within families and communities (Evans, 1993). They define what is OK for the young child, for example, passive girls/active boys, or the need for compulsory heterosexuality. Adult behaviour in children is condoned on the one hand by the appearance of adult looking child fashion models or childlike successful adult fashion models. However, the notion that minors might have any sexual feelings, even if they do not act upon them, is often repugnant. Sexual offenders, let us remember, frequently attribute adult motives and feelings to their victims, perhaps reflecting society's confusion about when a child is a child and what that period of a person's life contains.

In asking ourselves why such dichotomies are tolerated, we have to face our own investment in them. There is safety in our childhood images. Daddy's little girl may prefer to stay that way, rather than assume full adult responsibility. Even when our childhood images are unhealthy they may feel safer than change. Equally, our childhood experiences can be so damaging that change does not even get on the agenda.

Ultimately it is comforting to feel superior, or to belong. On a societal level it seems likely that the more a threatened culture or society is the less it can tolerate opposition. Power bases are underpinned by economic motives. Competition for scarce resources will lead to the development of distinct and strict rules for behaviour, often to the detriment of women or gays or sometimes those with different cultural heritage as the lives of the black citizens of this country will amply testify.

If society is comfortable there is little reason why you should question it. Consequently it is women who have developed feminism, black people who have been in the forefront of highlighting racism, and gays and lesbians who have been deconstructing images of appropriate sexual behaviour. One can also be 'bought off' from seeing one's own powerlessness as Angela Davis (1981) has suggested of the man who rapes. Thus heterosexual women engaging in conventional marriages have chosen to reap the fruits of male domination in subtle ways at the expense of other women. Using this analysis one could view abusers as trying to 'buy in' to power or authority as they are taught to understand it.

Society, we would suggest, is ambiguous in its statements to its members. It allows, in fact encourages, citizens to distance themselves from the unpleasant behaviour of others. It allows citizens not to see their part in the production of behaviour or that human behaviour is on a continuum. Much of the work of this book will be to outline the impact of such ambiguities on work to challenge behaviour and on the experience of workers.

Definitions

It is important to be clear about the meanings of words we use in a world where ambiguity is deliberately fostered. Sex and gender, for example, are words often used as if they are interchangeable. For the purposes of this work, gender refers to one's ascribed role as masculine or feminine. Sex refers to act or behaviour. Other working definitions that need exploring are those around sexuality. If we talk of gay men or lesbians we will be referring to their chosen identity. It is important therefore to separate social identity from activity. For example, men who have sex with men will not all identify with a gay social identity. They will, however, be touched by many of the concerns and stereotypes outlined earlier. They will often be active in self-censorship, and if ever their activities are discovered they will immediately become the most important feature for public analysis.

There is, in our society, the imposition of a majority definition of appropriate sexuality as well as appropriate sexual acts. It is important here to acknowledge the range of identities and to find a clear way of defining the positive, for self and society, as against the negative ones. This debate is particularly important around the age of consent for gay sex, or the rights of transgender people.

The impact of the majority view of appropriate sexuality, personal behaviour, the defensiveness and subtle power with which it is imposed, has lead to all other definitions being defined as 'not OK' and lumped together as abnormal. Instead, they must be analysed separately for their positive or negative components and most chapters will contain elements of this analysis and outline debates around it. If one is to engage in any kind of work to challenge behaviour, one has to have a frame of reference in which such things are explored fully and without recourse to stereotypical thinking.

Choice of behaviour or sexual identity is not a simple concept. It can be a positive affirmation, or a distorted one. It can be a best choice for the person, or a path that is determined by damage, power seeking or oppression. Putting a label on things suits the majority. Being a heterosexual man or a lesbian woman makes statements about the person, allows them to be classified by others, and allows access to roles, validations and support relationships. It also allows others to make judgements and assumptions about the person and to allow those judgements to be the primary force in assessing the person. There are also those who genuinely believe they have no choices, and those who feel that the label they are given does not fit, is unjustly sexualised or is unpleasant to acknowledge. Whether we enable people to challenge the images of the label, as with challenging racism, or force them to accept its connotations, as when working with rapists, finally depends on our definitions of the acceptability of the behaviours contained within it. It has been suggested to us that the younger generation now perceives less need for labels and has a more fluid concept of gender roles and sexual identity. We would applaud this but find little evidence of it. We work with the here and now and observe a world where inter-gender hostility, homophobia and racism are still part of everyday behaviour. We live and work also in a world where every practitioner has constantly to make such decisions about how to use labels. Thus the importance of this book, we believe, is in sharing experience.

Acceptable Behaviour

In the context of what has just been said, the final definition for this introduction to explore, is that of the notion of acceptable behaviour, what constitutes it and how is it explored. For the purposes of this book, whilst it will be seen that authors are challenging some current values, they all work with a shared baseline. Acceptable sexual behaviours and the formation of any identity or support group around it have to be based on consensuality and the absence of abusive behaviour.

This is a broad working definition, around the interpretation of which there will continue to be many debates; some of it conducted in these chapters. There are issues around legality and age for example; the age of consent for gay and heterosexual men has been unequal in British society. Outside the legal framework there are other debates to be heard .For example the nature of power and consent in a relationship between a 40-year-old and a 16-year-old of whatever sexual identity will be very different from that between two peers. Again, because of the structural power positions of the genders and socially constructed inter-gender hostility, relationships between gay men or lesbian couples are essentially more egalitarian than heterosexual ones but their issues may be obscured. The law provides us with a standard around which debates can centre. Can consent to pain be legitimate, for example, if it originates from damage to the person? Around the exercise of sexual behaviour and the formation of identities, there is much indoctrination, much societal investment, and much misinformation. Ultimately, we can probably only establish principles, broad consensus and questions for the future.

The task this book has set itself is to explore some of these debates in detail through an examination of the issues that the authors face daily as workers and citizens. These issues could be summarised as:

- Institutionalised sexism and inequality resulting in hostility between genders, abuse, partner violence, and rape.
- Compulsory definitions of appropriate sexuality and sexual behaviour with consequent fear of difference as a challenge to power bases.
- The establishment of a power base through use of sexual behaviour in child abuse, abusive marriages and rape.
- The obscuring of issues of defining responsible behaviour and consensuality by the use of scapegoats and distancing.
- Refusals to acknowledge questions, or hear challenge, or accept experience if it counters the prevailing norms.
- Helpful and unhelpful laws and their application with stereotypical 'discretion.'

- The struggle for workers in deconstructing conventional wisdom and the often unsupported journey this entails.

The authors will present their work and personal experiences in the hope of stimulating further debate around these issues. For them the paramount aim is that of the desire to produce best practice whether it be in empowerment of the disadvantaged or challenge to the unacceptable. Their desire is to connect across boundaries. Hopefully by drawing the themes together we can, in conclusion, offer an analysis for the future. As editors we hope finally to offer a synthesis and a way forward.

References

Davis, A. (1981) *Women, Race and Class*. New York: Random House.

Dobash, R.E. and Dobash, R.P. (1992) *Women, Violence and Social Change*. London: Routledge.

Evans, D.T. (1993) *Sexual Citizenship*. London: Routledge.

Hill Collins, P. (1991) *Black Feminist Thought*. London: Routledge.

Srage, L. (1997) Should Feminists Oppose Prostitution? In Gruen, L. and Panichas, G. *Sex, Morality and the Law*. London: Routledge.

CHAPTER 2

'Stranger Danger': Some Problems with Community Notification

Michelle Meloy

This chapter based on a North American experience will seek to evidence that a refusal to explore the reality of perpetrator's experience, leads to 'quick fit' solutions which are themselves risky and counter-productive in any long term goal of creating a safer community.

No criminal provokes more interest or intrigue than the sex offender. The topic has generated volumes of research. The media rarely misses an opportunity to capitalise on a titillating and sensational sexual assault headline. These stories provide the necessary ingredients to captivate an audience: sex, trauma, grief, taboo. The media often accentuates instances where the assailant is an unknown predator or stranger to the victim.

Sensational media coverage, although not inherently inaccurate, is haphazard and reckless, contributing to misplaced fear and a distorted image of offence patterns and offender characteristics. These stories convey the message that danger lurks *solely* beyond the confines of one's front door, but never within it. Furthermore, the reporting of these dramatic, albeit statistically rare, stranger danger sexual attacks engenders a moral panic, and facilitates the unprecedented speed at which sex offender laws have passed through state and federal legislatures. Whether or not these legal actions, including sex offender registration and community notification, are *good* social policy remains to be seen. But, certainly this agenda on sex offenders feeds the public appetite for retribution and public shaming.

Community notification policies, fueled by emotion and fear, have been presented to the public as the 'cure-all'. Supporters of these laws claim that mandatory sex offender registration and community notification provide the 'safety blanket' to keep children and neighbourhoods free from sexual predators. Academics speculate over the concerns and questions hovering around community notification. The media bombards us with images of strangers lurking in the dark. Politicians rhapsodise over the law's 'promise' and virtuousness, (Finn, 1997; Brooks, 1996; Berliner, 1996; Prentky, 1996; Lieb, 1996; Myers, 1996; Steinbock, 1995; Freeman-Longo, 1996) yet the legislation remains untested. The lack of thorough evaluations makes it impossible to know whether community notification laws will curb sexual offending behaviour. As a result, the community is left to wonder if this is merely 'feel-good' legislation.

In 1995, the single empirical study was published on the topic. It explored the impact of community notification on sexual offending recidivism and found it produced no statistically significant difference in re-arrest rates (Schram and Millor, 1995). Registered sex offenders were just as likely to be arrested for new sex crimes as they were before the law was implemented. This ethnographic research involved convicted male sex offenders who described, in their own words, how they define themselves, their crimes, community notification and their status as sexual deviants.

Literature suggests there is a gender difference in how men and women view, construct and experience situations (Scully, 1991). As a result, females are unable to explain the thought processes and rationalisations of sexually violent men because men and women have different visions or reality of the situation. Therefore, the words of male sex offenders are needed to demystify their thought processes and perceptions. Furthermore, sex offending is a gendered crime. Known perpetrators are overwhelmingly male while victims are overwhelmingly female. In essence, this chapter will examine males who sexually violate females.[1] It is an attempt to delve into the heads and minds of male sex offenders. Additionally, in an effort to 'peel back the layers' of official protocol, it will critically examine how the American criminal justice system identifies, defines, processes, and labels male sex offenders.

Definition of the Situation

'If men define situations as real, they are real in their consequences' (Thomas, 1928) Offenders' own words and perceptions may teach us a great deal about their behaviour. How an individual defines a situation is central to how that individual behaves. Although perceptions may be inaccurate, they determine what people actually do. For instance, if I perceive my neighbour to be a 'perverted, sick, child molester', even though this reality may be incorrect, my definition of this situation may dictate specific actions on my behalf about this particular neighbour.

Labelling

The Construction of a 'Deviant'
Contrary to popular belief, deviance does not 'just happen'. It is something actively made or created. Someone or some process has to pass judgment, or, stigmatise, for deviance to occur. The creation of crime and deviance is a

---

[1] Although nearly all of the research subjects reported having only female victims some of the offenders stated they had a history of offending males and females or males only.

complex social process. It involves the decisions, interpretations, beliefs, and actions of a 'professional class of deviant producers' with varying degrees of power and authority dictating problematic behaviour (Sumner, 1994, p215).

The underlying premise in the labelling paradigm is that deviance is socially constructed. The media, government, public and social control agents are all active players in the building process. What we identity as a social problem is essentially a collection of subjective definitions of 'bad' as opposed to an objective social measure of what is inherently harmful or immoral (Blumer, 1971). Deviance is not self-evident. There is no 'deviance gauge' to identify those who are clearly bad or clearly evil. Accordingly, labelling theorists (Tannenbaum, 1938; Lemert, 1951; Becker, 1963; Cohen, 1955) focus on the social role through which informal and formal stigmatic labels are applied. In labelling theory, attention is focused *away* from the behaviour itself and *toward* the process by which an act becomes labelled as criminal or deviant.

Society typically proclaims the sexual norm violator to be a deviant. Deviance categories have changed over time, reflecting the elastic notion of what sexual acts are considered acceptable and what acts are viewed as obscene or immoral. Importantly, the 'sex offender' label assists in objectifying and dehumanising that which we do not like or understand. Placing stigmatic labels allows *us* to distance ourselves from *them*. Sex offenders become officially constructed as dangerous, deviant, and folk devils, enabling them to be construed as 'thing-like' and reified as enemies. The act of reification entails conceptualising an abstraction as if it had real or concrete properties. 'When a concept is reified, or given a life of its own, we tend to forget the extent to which our own beliefs and actions contribute to the construction and perpetuation of the process . . .' (O'Brien and Kollack, 1996, p37).

Labelling theory suggests that the placing of the stigma is what positions the individual at a greater risk for re-offending. In other words, the individual's acceptance of the 'criminal' or 'deviant' label and the subsequent adherence to it, promotes future criminal acts. Theorists argue that the deviance which occurred prior to the label was unsystematic, unorganised and sporadic; rather, it is the societal reaction which is the propelling force leading the individual into further deviant behaviour. To recap, being caught, publicly labelled, and ritually constructed as a deviant is an essential component in the process of creating a pattern of criminal or deviant behaviour. Whether a person accepts this path depends primarily on how others, especially agents of social control, respond to him/her (Becker, 1963, pp31–32).

Community Notification Laws

The 'Bad Man' Mindset

The first community notification legislation in USA was enacted in Washington state in 1990 after the sexual assault and mutilation of a young Tacoma boy. Four years later, in 1994, the horrific rape and murder of a seven-year-old New Jersey girl by her neighbour, a twice-convicted sexual offender, rocked the nation. These tragedies led to the enactment of mandatory registration and community notification laws targeting sex offenders, commonly referred to as Megan's Law, named after the New Jersey victim, Megan Kanka. This package of sex offender statutes was proposed to better protect the community, specifically children, by mandating convicted sex offenders to register with their local law enforcement agencies upon conviction or release. The most sensitive and controversial aspect of the law, however, is community notification, whereby information about the offender's name and residence is made readily available to the public. In some instances, the offender's picture, work address, residence and details about the crime are available everywhere from highway bill-boards to the internet 'super highway.' Due to the growing number of web sites posting sex offender information, as more citizens become technologically proficient, details will become but a computer-key-stroke away. Also, in some states, such as Delaware, the defendant's driver's licence contains a special mark designating him/her as a sexual offender. The invasive labelling of sex offenders is necessary, according to Mrs. Kanka, because, '. . . if I had known that three sex perverts were living across the street from me, Megan would be alive today' (Steinbock, 1995, p7).

Mrs Kanka is not alone in her belief that a sex offender's information should be accessible to the public. The support for this legislation is demonstrated not only by the swift passage of Megan's Law itself (which the state of New Jersey adopted only weeks after Megan's murder) but also by the fact that within the same year 16 other states had written similar policies. In 1996 the United States congress passed legislation which required all states to have some form of community notification for convicted sex offenders (Finn, 1997, p3). As of the end of 1998, all 50 states have sex offender registration laws, 48 of which already carry a community notification mandate. A constant stream of legal challenges is unlikely to end until, and unless, the highest court in the nation, the United States Supreme Court, hears the issue and rules definitively on the constitutionality of these laws which, to date, they have refused to do.

Notwithstanding its obvious public and political support, community notification will not and *can not* stop sexual attacks. Additionally, the legislation introduces an abundance of potential complications. For instance, sex offender registration and community notification have been successful at the legislative level *not* because it has been proved to be good crime control but 'because it is good politics' says Walter Dickey, 'if our courts would recognize all this vote-crazed legislation for what it is, there could be a more civilized approach and less criminal sexual conduct as a result' (National Center for Institutions and Alternatives, 1996, p11).

Community notification is an administrative and implementation nightmare. Collection, maintenance, enforcement, and sex offender notification to the community is expensive, labour intensive, and likely to be incomplete and inaccurate as offenders may change residences frequently or refuse to co-operate (Freeman-Longo, 1996; Lieb, 1996; Prentky, 1996; Steinbock, 1995). For instance, because of the stigma associated with community notification, offenders often move to other communities and may not notify officials of the change. One study conducted in Tennessee revealed that 28 per cent of convicted sex offenders moved from their registered communities and then failed to re-register (Finn, 1997, p16). Not only is community notification costly in terms of finances and resources but the legislation itself may lead to society paying the ultimate price in the form of additional victims. Since sex offender registration and community notification target the 'stranger' sexual assailant scenario and make no provisions to protect children who fall prey to sexual offences in their own home, they create and present an inaccurate image of children's sexual victimisation. Conservative estimates indicate that between 75–89 per cent of child sexual abuse is committed by family members and friends (Steinbock, 1995, p5). Consequently, sex offender registration laws imbue a false sense of security by leading communities into the 'big, bad man mindset.' Most child molesters are not crazed, savage, beast-like strangers. Quite the contrary. Many sex offenders hold positions of authority and are relatives or acquaintances of the child, *not* strangers (Quindlen, 1994).

Another logistical complication of sex offender legislation involves the volume of offenders who are able to escape notification requirements through plea negotiations. It is common practice for offenders to enter into plea negotiations for offences which do not carry the registration mandate. A 'successful' plea agreement does not negate an offender's potential to sexually re-offend. Many of the non-mandated registrants may be equally dangerous if not more dangerous than registered offenders (Freeman-Longo, 1996, p99). For example, Richard Allen Davis, the individual convicted in California of the highly publicised sexual assault and murder of Polly Klaas, had previously served fifteen years in prison for sex crimes, dating back to 1973. However, because of plea negotiations he was able to avoid convictions for the specific sex offences, which would have required him to register (Steinbock, 1995, p5). Furthermore, as disturbing as it is to do so, it must be acknowledged that since sex crimes are severely underreported and few offenders are ever caught, registration legislation applies to only the *small percentage* of offenders who are identified, apprehended and convicted of committing sex crimes.

Finally, and directly related to other themes raised in this chapter, is the question of what overall impact the labelling and public branding of an individual as 'sex offender' is likely to have. There is no empirical evidence this legislation makes children safer. Some experts believe the stigmatising effects of community notification will actually *increase* the number of sexual assaults. For instance, the notification process may further alienate the offender, increasing feelings of detachment, anger and making it more difficult for registered offenders to find housing and employment thereby enhancing their likelihood of sexual re-offending (Hall, Nagayama and Proctor, 1987; Furby *et al.*, 1989; Hanson *et al.*, 1995; National Center for Institutions and Alternatives, 1996). There is also an increased risk of attack by vigilantes.

Offenders and their Experience of Registration

In-depth, ethnographic interviews were conducted with 20 convicted sex offenders in a Midwestern (USA) county during the months of January, 1997 through September, 1997. All participants matched a specific profile:

- male
- currently on felony probation
- court-mandated into sex offender specific treatment
- required to register as a sex offender with local law enforcement.

My position as a probation officer within the Court Services Division of that Midwestern county government provided me with access to research subjects.

Survey participants were advised of this research project by their sex offender therapist. Participation was conducted on a strictly volunteer basis. Subjects were actively enrolled in sex offender therapy at one of three local treatment facilities. The research volunteers were fully informed of the academic nature of the study and they were guaranteed confidentiality with regard to their personal identities. 20 of the 74 sex offenders invited agreed to participate in the study. There was little differentiation among the sample in terms of ethnicity and sexual orientation. Most of the research subjects were white while three were of Hispanic origin. Two of the subjects defined themselves as homosexual while the others described themselves as heterosexual (interestingly this self definition did not always correlate with the gender of their victim). The age group of the sample ranged from 19 to 60. The offenders covered the gamut in terms of socio-economic status, employment and professional occupations and educational attainment.

Although there were a few exceptions, the research volunteers were considered to be 'in-compliance' with their probation and treatment requirements.

One can only speculate as to what prompted these men to engage in the research process. Perhaps, despite affirmations otherwise, they believed their decision to participate would be viewed favourably by the practitioners and courts working with them. It is also likely they viewed the project as a rare opportunity to 'speak out' about their situation and treatment by the criminal justice system. Interview questions focused on how the individual defined and experienced his label as a sex offender. Due to the limited number of interviews conducted, caution must be exercised in generalising specific findings of this research but it may shed light on the issue of how sex offenders define, interpret, and experience their stigmatic label.

Results

Neutralising Definitions

Sykes and Matza (1957) introduced techniques of neutralisation or 'learned excuses' which illustrates how individuals are able to violate societal norms without necessitating a total rejection of the norms themselves. In essence, the process of 'neutralization' enables one to justify that which otherwise would be unacceptable behaviour. These rationalisations were frequently used by sex offenders to justify their actions. An example of a 'neutralisation' definition is illustrated in the following dialogue. This individual's conviction is for possession of child pornography. The subject translates this 'hands-off', that is, possession of child pornography crime, into a 'victimless' act via neutralisation:

> *It would be nice if I wasn't labelled as a sex offender since I don't have a victim . . . there was no physical contact anywhere.*

He continues to use neutralising definitions in his description of an incident involving sexual activities which occurred between a young boy and a middle-aged man.

> *I mean, even if the sex act itself did not harm the child, if it came out in public, then the public's view would harm the child.*

> *Some guy was on trial and he had a loving and consensual relationship with a boy.*

For another interviewee, being a 'sex offender' is particularly troublesome because he believes society reserves its deepest resentment for sex offenders. He defined sexual criminals as being at the bottom of the 'criminal hierarchy':

17

Being a sex offender is probably the most taboo thing you can be, you know, in society. And people frown on it a lot more, than say if I was a murderer. Sex offenders are probably on the . . . bottom of the food chain, as far as criminals go, I guess.

Another man described the 'unsavory' way he believes sex offenders are viewed and treated by the judicial system.

Sex criminals are put into a category that seems to be unclean, you know, the court treats them in that way.

Because sex offenders are involved in issues of morality much more closely observed by society. When you offend that kind of close moral conviction by society, you come off as being more deviant. People that break into houses to steal property are obviously criminals, but they are not deviant.

This man continued:

So I didn't do anything violent to anybody, and had no history of doing anything violent to anybody and I'm not ever going to do anything violent to anybody, but because I was a sex criminal, I was bonded out for ten thousand dollars more than this guy who attacked a police officer with a deadly weapon.

His description is an example of neutralisation where he refuses to equate sex with violence. The defendant's claim that he 'didn't do anything violent' is a justification for why he considers his crime, i.e., deviant sex acts, less severe than the man charged with allegedly attacking a police officer.

The power of stigma is portrayed in the following example where the subject attempts to manage the impression he gives of himself, including to his family, employer, and police, via his presentation as something other than a sex offender. Neutralisation is accomplished by accepting the less stigmatising and damaging label of 'felon' in place of 'sex offender.'

I think that like, stealing a car, for instance, is the kind of thing you could almost brag about. I mean, granted yes, it's wrong, it's a crime, but it is something . . . I would not mind admitting that to you or anybody else. I mean like, hey I, took it for a joy ride or whatever, what the hell! You know. Compared to, oh, hey, I sexually offended somebody.

or by denial . . .

I guess I could say I'm pretty honest and open about it, but you know like people I know on a bowling league, hell, I won't tell them . . . they'll judge me . . . everybody whispering behind my back and pointing their finger and look'n at me, I don't want that.

It is clear that these offenders believe, and perhaps rightly so, that society views them as repugnant. Their recognition and internalisation of their low social-standing leads them to the use of neutralisations and rationalisations to justify their sexually deviant behaviour.

Community Notification . . . in neon lights

Mandatory registration and community notification are included in the interviews because they are central to understanding how the respondents experience the label of a sex offender.[2] It is possible that the offenders' interpretations reflect the current social times. For instance, had this research been undertaken fifteen or twenty years ago, prior to the implementation of these laws and the stigmatisation which followed, the respondents might present very different descriptions of their experience as a 'sex offender'. Although this data cannot provide evidence of recidivism following the enactment of community notification laws, it does provide offenders' accounts on how *they* see the new laws affecting their thought processes and behaviour. Offenders were asked to define 'community notification' and to speculate on the law's ability to affect recidivism.

> *Registration . . . if you have a felony charge, you have to register with your local police department and township . . . that you're a sex offender . . . that you're a sex deviant.*

> *Like registration . . . registration is for 10 years, and you have to do it and pay for a crime for 10 years.*

> *Registration? That's awful humiliating to go down there, every year . . . to the police department . . . and say ah, I'm a sex offender.*

Based on these and other like observations, it is obvious these sex offenders understand what the law is designed to accomplish. However, they also find the process humiliating and often unrelated to future offending.

Public Denunciation

It makes me feel as if I am already dead

Degradation ceremonies (Garfinkle, 1965, p421) are an integral component to the criminal justice system. Public denunciation and degradation create a social response toward the offender such as the sentencing hearing in which the judge imposes punishment. If the person is found to have committed a

---

[2]Mandatory registration and community notification are terms that are often used interchangeably. But, this was not always the case. For instance, the state of California has had legislation on their criminal law books for over twenty years which required the mandatory registration of all convicted sex offenders; information which was available to law enforcement only. However, due to legislative changes, mandatory registration and community notification have become 'meshed' to the point where making distinctions between the two is nearly impossible.

violation of the law they are 'ritually destroyed.' Their identity is transformed and replaced by another. The perpetrator becomes a different person, a 'reconstituted' person, a guilty person, in this case: a sexual deviant. Although not a quantative assessment the research allows, perhaps for the first time, sex offenders to comment on community notification's likelihood to make a difference in their own behaviour as follows:

For a long time I had this label across my forehead, on my back, said sex offender, you know, like in neon lights . . . you have to convince yourself that, yeah, I've done my time and I am doing what I'm supposed to be doing, I'm going through treatment, I'm learning, I know, **I know** *(emphasis added) in my heart that I am never going to do that again, it's a real hard penalty, the registration.*

Registration . . . it makes you feel like a total outcast. It makes me feel like a piece of dirt. This label . . . it makes me feel as if I am already dead.

I really believe it is not protecting the neighbourhood. It just causes hate and discontentment in the neighbourhood.

It strikes me that registration requirements for sex offenders has no hope of being effective at anything. So, to have someone give up their constitutional rights in a process that has no hope of being effective at preventing anything, seems a very misguided step.

People who are going to act out are going to act out . . . just because I went into a police station and registered does not mean I am not going to act . . . nobody sat back and said, okay, now let's see . . . how can we protect our children? How can we reduce recidivism? Let's have people register. **That is not** *(emphasis added) what happened. Even if he is registered in all 50 states in every county, every community, every hamlet, that is* **still** *(emphasis added) not going to prevent a person who is going to offend, from going out and offending . . . it is irrational.*

I don't necessarily think it will make it more difficult to re-offend. No, I don't think it will.

Bluntly, no it will not work. I do not think my name being on a list, one way or the other, would deter future commissions of crime. That is just putting it bluntly. I am looking inward at myself, and, I am already on a list. What the heck difference does it make to me if I go out and commit another crime? So no, I do not believe it would be a deterrent at all.

Nothing in my behaviour has changed because of registration, except that I had to go and pay $10.00 and register.

Megan's Law will give you a guarantee ... but if it is going to happen, Megan's Law is not going to stop it. If someone is set on harming a child, I don't think that any law in the world is going to change it ... It will limit access (to victims) immensely. But again, if the person is dead set on doing to a child, he will. He will figure out a way ...

This law will probably not make a difference, when you get to that point ... to go out and do something like that, I don't think you give a damn about what happens.

The list needs to be used as a proper tool to keep the community safe. Okay, the police officer has a gun. You don't just give everyone else a gun and say you can have this and it will make you safe.

A person who has committed manslaughter is a danger to his community just like a person who committed a rape or an abduction or a molestation. I think we should be consistent and if we are going to register criminals, let's register all of them.

Once again, offenders distinctly hone in on the stigmatising, alienating, and ostracising components to community notification. And, they offer speculation to the effect that community notification will be far more effective at labelling than it will be at reducing the risks of sexual victimisation.

Results

This research examined how convicted male sex offenders experience their deviant label. To that end, subjects were questioned regarding their definitions of their crime, label, community notification and themselves. Participation in the study was strictly voluntary, which introduces the possibility of a biased sample. It is unlikely that individuals who were performing poorly on probation and/or in sex offender therapy would be eager to volunteer, thereby creating a skewed sample. It is also worthwhile to consider the extent to which offenders reported their 'true' perceptions, as well as what their participation motives may have been. Finally, it would be interesting to know what (if any) effect the therapist may have had on each group member's decision as to whether or not to participate. Despite these potential limitations this study *gets into the heads and minds* of sex offenders by letting them speak for themselves. Their words reveal an insight into the crimes and thought processes of sexual offenders.

Collectively, research subjects perceived themselves as a stigmatised group of offenders and as such could be seen using impression management techniques as a remedial action to the stigmatic label associated with their sex crimes. In most instances, community notification laws were cited as the overriding source of the stigma. Respondents discussed what they believed to be the socially constructed nature of their crimes in light of recent social pressures and judicial prioritisation on sexual offending laws. Several offenders commented on the 'disproportionately severe' criminal justice sanctions levied against sexual crime perpetrators relevant to the 'lenient' sentences imposed for other types of violent criminal acts.

Participants believed that both the judicial system and the public viewed sexual offenders far more negatively than they viewed other types of offenders. As a result, research subjects constructed a myriad of neutralising definitions in an effort to present themselves in a more favourable light. Subjects often went to great lengths to cast themselves as anything but the 'typical' (i.e. the enemy) sex offender.

Without exception, subjects supported mandatory registration, but denounced making the information available for public view. All the offenders proclaimed they had no intention to re-offend sexually. However, they also stated that community notification would in no way inhibit their ability or desire to do so. Supporters of the legislation may respond 'I don't care what these offenders think or feel about community notification (or anything for that matter). If my neighbour is a sex offender I want to know.' One inherent flaw in this argument is the underlying assumption that all sex offenders are caught and convicted, when in reality 'known' offenders make up only a small portion of those actually committing sex crimes. Steinbock (1995, p8) asserts:

> . . . *we should not ask what people are likely to want to know, but rather, ask what are the effects of community notification? If it does not increase safety and instead promotes a false sense of security . . . we need to find more effective, less dangerous ways of achieving the paramount goal of protecting children.*

Discussion

The results of this study suggest some policy recommendations. First, if sex offender registration continues, it should be revised in order to reflect a greater range of offences. A 'successful' plea negotiation does not in and of itself eliminate or reflect the potential dangerousness of an individual.

Second, some states have incorporated a tier system into their community notification legislation in an attempt to assess an offender's potential risk to the community. The 'tier system' classifies the offender's potential for re-offending into one of three classes: low, medium, or high and regulates the degree of community notification accordingly. There continues to be debate over the constitutionality and effectiveness of tier systems.

Predictions of future behaviour are common practice by the criminal justice system and a necessary component to this policy. However, the ability to accurately predict future behaviour is a dubious undertaking where over prediction is the norm. The presumption that law enforcement officials can 'just know' who will re-offend is a myth. In other words, the unpredictability of human actions makes it impossible to determine who is dangerous and who is not. In short, 'predicting what one convicted offender will do in the next few weeks or months is impossible'. For instance, the accuracy of predictions of future dangerousness, or the likelihood of re-offence, is often no better than 30 per cent accurate (Steinbock, 1995, p5).

Third, policy agenda question surrounds the logic of 'singling' out sex criminals (Freeman-Longo, 1996, p98). If society is concerned about dangerous offenders and crime, why not notify the public about the release of all offenders including murderers, drug dealers, and other violent criminals? Is it due to the belief that sex offenders have higher re-offence rates than other types of assailants? If the rationale for not having all 'dangerous' criminals register relies upon the differentiation of re-offence rates perhaps policy makers should rethink this position. Researchers can not conclude with any degree of certainty the extent to which convicted sex offenders re-offend. A review of the literature indicates that sex offenders who have been formally processed (i.e. apprehended, convicted) have a *much lower* sexual recidivism rate (roughly 13 per cent) than previously thought (Hanson and Bussiere, 1998; National Center for Institutions and Alternatives, 1996; Furby *et al.*, 1989). One would suspect recidivism to be higher for unidentified offenders, however. After all, their offending behaviour, by definition, is unknown to agents of social control so it is unlikely they are receiving treatment services of other forms of intervention nor will their name appear on any sex offender registration list.

Fourth, dissemination of sex offender registration lists should be reserved for criminal justice personnel. Not only is community notification near the bounds of constitutionality but there is no empirical data to support the efficacy of the legisla ion. The only known scholarly inquiry on the topic showed no statisticaly significant difference in recidivism rates after the implementation of community notifications laws (Washington State Institute for Public Policy, 1995). Furthermore, this legislation does nothing to ensure the safety of those who are victimised by 'familiar hands', i.e. family members and friends. Roughly 80–85 per cent of all sexual assault victims fall prey to this form of sexual exploitation. Not only does community notification encourage a 'false sense of security' the legislation *creates* and *promotes* a distorted picture of where (and by whom) the greatest sexual victimisation dangers lies (Quindlen, 1994).

To increase public awareness, more education on the topic of sex crimes is needed. Both children and adults need to be well informed regarding the dynamics of sexual offending as this is perhaps the best way to help ensure one's safety against a sexual assault. This is particularly important as most people harbour the misconception that sexual offenders are strangers (i.e. 'stranger danger'). The best way to keep children safe is by teaching them reasonable safety rules (Steinbock, 1995, p7).

Fifth, treatment for sex offenders should be mandatory for all individuals convicted of a sexually related offence. Failure to fully comply with treatment should be met with stringent court reprisal. Studies support the effectiveness of sex offender therapy for reducing sexual recidivism. The re-offence rate for offenders who completed cognitively-based sex offender treatment is found to be half that of offenders who did not engage in such therapy. Additional studies have provided optimism for the effectiveness of sex offender treatment in lowering sexual recidivism rates for offenders (Hanson and Bussiere, 1998; National Center for Institutions and Alternatives, 1996; Becker, 1963; Margues *et al.*, 1994; Marshal *et al.*, 1991). Not only does some research demonstrate that sex offender treatment is correlated with lower recidivism rates, but it is also more cost effective than other types of intervention such as incarceration. Research participants in this study voiced their support of the treatment process and cited it as the predominant factor in controlling their sexual deviance.

Finally, specialised sex offender supervision units should be utilised for offenders serving their sentence in the community. Research findings suggest that effective community based supervision, such as with specially trained probation and/or parole officers, is one of the best, and cheapest, defences in combating sexual victimisation (Cumming and Buell, 1997; and Berliner *et al.*, 1995). Since treating and supervising sex offenders in the community is only pennies to the dollar compared to the astronomical cost of herding people in prison cells, properly training community based agents makes much more sense than resorting to a prison building frenzy.

This chapter has accentuated existing gaps in the literature as it pertains to male sexual offenders' interpretations relating to their own sexual offending, and how the American criminal justice system has responded to the male sexual offender, particularly in terms of labelling. The importance of male sex offender interpretations should not be understated because the offenders' definition of a situation may be the driving force for future actions. And, as stated earlier, since sex offending is a gendered phenomenon where males hold a near monopoly on offending and females on the role of victim: a glimpse into the construction of the 'reality' of sexually violent men can prove beneficial to understanding their world and challenging their distortions. Therefore, it would be short sighted for any society that proclaims a desire to end sexual victimisation to ignore the perceptions of the actual offenders. Furthermore, a probe of the social process by which individuals come to be identified and labelled as deviant is critical to enhancing our understanding of how sex offenders are ritually assembled and socially constructed. The label 'deviant' is reserved for something or someone deemed socially unacceptable. This chapter seeks, not to rebuke the social definition of 'appropriate' sexual behaviour but rather to acknowledge that it is, in fact, a *process*, not a 'given', and to pose questions as to society's motives for emphasising it as 'fact'. I wish I had the answers on what the long-term effects and implications will be for publicly branding sex offenders. I wish someone would ask the question.

References

Becker, H. (1963) *Outsiders: Studies of Sociology of Deviance*. New York: Free Press.

Becker, J. and Hunter, J.A. Jr. (1992) Evaluation of Treatment Outcome for Adult Perpetrators of Child Sexual Abuse. *Criminal Justice and Behaviour*. V:19(1): pp74–92.

Berliner, L. (1996) Commentary: Community Notification of Sex Offenders. *Journal of Interpersonal Violence*. V:11(2): pp294–295.

Berliner, L., Schram, D., Miller, L. and Milloy, C. (1995) A Sentencing Alternative for Sex Offenders: A Study of Decision Making and Recidivism. *Journal of Interpersonal Violence*. V:10(4): pp487–502.

Blumer, H. (1971) *Symbolic Interactionism: Perspective and Method*. Englewood Cliffs, New Jersey: Prentice.

Brooks, A. (1996) Meagan's Law: Constitutionality and Policy. *Criminal Justice Ethics*. V:14(2): pp56–66.

Cohen, A.K. (1955) *Delinquent Boys*. Glencoe, IL: Free Press.

Cumming, G. and Buell, M. (1997) *Supervision of the Sex Offender*. Brandon, Vt: Safer Society Press.

Finn, P. (1997) Sex Offender Community Notification. *National Institute of Justice*. V:35: pp1–32.

Freeman-Longo. (1996) Feel Good Legislation: Prevention or Calamity. *Child Abuse and Neglect*. V:(2): pp95–101.

Furby, L., Blackshaw, L. and Weinrott, M. (1989) Sex Offender Recidivism: A Review. *Psychological Bulletin*. V:105(1): pp3–30.

Garfinkle, H. (1965) Conditions of Successful Degradation Ceremonies. *American Journal of Sociology*. V:61: pp420–424.

Hall-Nagayama, G. and Proctor, W. (1987) Criminological Predictors of Recidivism in a Sexual Offender Population. *Journal of Consulting and Clinical Psychology*. V:55(1): pp111–112.

Hanson, R.K. and Bussiere, M. (1998) Predicting Relapse: A Meta-Analysis of Sexual Offender Recidivism Studies. *Journal of Counseling and Clinical Psychology*. V:66(2): pp348–362.

Hanson, R., Scott, H. and Steffy, R. (1995) A Comparison of Child Molesters and Nonsexual Criminals: Risk Predictors and Long-term Recidivism. *Journal of Research in Crime and Delinquency.* V:32(3): pp325–337.

Lieb, R. (1996) Commentary: Community Notification Laws: A Step Toward More Effective Solutions. *Journal of Interpersonal Violence.* V:11(2): pp298–300.

Lemert, E. (1951) *Social Pathology.* New York: McGraw-Hill.

Assessment and Treatment of Sex Offenders: A Comprehensive Victim-Oriented Approach. *Journal of Offender Rehabilitation.* V:22(1/2): pp77–96.

Lemert, E. (1997) *The Trouble with Evil: Social Control at the Edge of Morality.* New York: State University of New York Press.

Marshal, W.L., Jones, R., Ward, A., Johnston, P. and Barbaree, H.E. (1991) Treatment Outcome with Sex Offenders. *Clinical Psychology Review.* V:11: pp465–485.

Margues, J., Day, D., Nelson, C. and West, A. (1994) Effects of Cognitive-Behavioral Treatment on Sex Offender Recidivism. *Criminal Justice and Behavior.* V:21(1): pp28–54.

Myers, J. (1996) Commentary: Societal Self-Defense: New Laws to Protect Children From Sexual Abuse. *Child Abuse and Neglect.* V:20(4): pp255–258.

National Center for Institutions and Alternatives. (1996) *Community Notification and Setting the Record Straight on Recidivism.*

O'Brien, J. and Kollack, P. (1996) *The Production of Reality: Essays and Readings on Social Interaction.* 2nd Edition. Thousand Oaks, California: Pine Forge.

Prentky, R. (1996) Commentary: Community Notification and Constructive Risk Assessment. *Journal of Interpersonal Violence.* V:11(2): pp295–298.

Quindlen. (1994) So, What if Law Isn't Fair to Sex Offenders? Children Come First. *Chicago Tribune,* August 8 pA13.

Schram, D. and Millor, C. (1995) Community Notification: A Study of Offender Characteristics and Recidivism. *Washington State Institute for Public Policy:* Seattle, WA: Urban Policy Research.

Scully, D. (1991) *Understanding Sexual Violence: A Study of Convicted Rapists.* London: HarperCollins.

Steinbock, B. (1995) Commentaries on the Issue. *Criminal Justice Ethics.* V:14: pp4–9.

Sumner, C. (1994) *The Sociology of Deviance: An Obituary.* New York: Continuum Press.

Sykes, G. and Matza, D. (1957) Techniques of Neutralization: A Theory of Delinquency. *American Journal of Sociology.* V:22: pp664–670.

Tannenbaum, F. (1938) *Crime and the Community.* New York: Columbia University Press.

Thomas, W.I. (1928) *The Child in America.* New York: Knopf.

CHAPTER 3

Sexuality and Sex Offending

Jo Thompson and Victoria Hodgett

This chapter discusses the impact of issues of sexuality on the approach to therapeutic interventions with sex offenders, and the impact of working with sex offenders, on the sexuality and self image of probation staff who engage in the work. It is based on the authors' extensive work experience both as practitioners and staff supervisors. It ends with some pointers for change and, of necessity, poses questions about the lack of awareness that has been displayed to these issues in the past.

Introduction

The aim of this chapter is to open up a discussion on the fundamental interconnectedness between the sexual life histories, sense of self and sexual identity of the worker, and the offender. We believe that this discourse is, in itself, defined by contemporary values and exists within a culture which we need to understand, before we can begin to work within it without being damaged by that work. We focus therefore on the context, within which sex offenders are defined as such, and within which offenders and workers struggle to retain a sense of self and a sexual identity. In so doing we may begin to explain the nature of the dilemmas presented by the work rather than explain the work itself.

This is not a brief practice guide: there are a number of highly competent practice manuals that have been published by practitioners and academics. This is instead one attempt to open up a debate, and perhaps to instigate an examination of the personal consequences for staff who do the work. Working with sex offenders probes the core of the offenders themselves, and it challenges the workers' sense of identity and self worth. The impact is experienced differently, depending on the gender, sexual orientation, life and sexual histories of the workers. In the latter section of this chapter we thus intend to focus on the nature of this impact on them.

In 1998, HM Inspectorate of Probation published a report of an inspection they had undertaken on the probation service's work with sex offenders. It was called *Exercising constant vigilance: The Role of the Probation Service in Protecting the Public from Sex Offenders* (Home Office, 1998). The title itself is quite emotive, it demonstrates some of the burden of responsibility felt by

27

staff for keeping people safe, and the guilt felt when another offence is committed. Probation officers have been developing therapeutic interventions with sex offenders, with little support or resources, since the early 1980s, but as the HMIP report points out, it is only comparatively recently that this area of offending has been intensively reported.

One result of this is that probation staff are expected, unrealistically, to protect the public and are pilloried if they fail to do so. The report makes recommendations on best practice, organisation and training: it touches very peripherally on the personal needs of staff for support, counselling, debriefing and survival. Indeed it does not speak about the issues of the recruitment and selection of staff and the need for staff to opt into the work rather than be directed to undertake it. These omissions may be about resourcing, i.e. they are not affordable and thus not to be mentioned. However they may also be about how these issues are seen and whether they are acknowledged as issues at all.

It is interesting that when the prison service took on the overwhelming need to engage in work with sex offenders in custody, it was properly resourced; programmes were researched and designed; best practice was integral and staff were recruited, vetted, supported, counselled and valued. Much of the prison's sex offending treatment programme owes its expertise to the probation service. In terms of recognition of the pioneering work done by staff, there has been little. There has been no recognition at all of the damage done to individual staff who have had to find their own means of survival. This work has the capacity to destroy our sense of self worth, our ability to express ourselves sexually; to make us question our sexual feelings and responses to others; and ultimately to destroy relationships or our capacity to form trusting relationships with others.

The Context

Sex offenders are categorised by their contravention of a number of laws, constructed historically by white, heterosexual institutions. Sex offenders are also labelled and demonised by other institutions, individuals and groups who would wish to set themselves apart from these offenders: their abnormality is useful in defining others' normality or 'OK-ness' or decency. Sex offenders as beasts and perverts are thus socially constructed; they are defined as such within a legislative code constructed by a dominant white, male, heterosexist ideology.

Probation staff who devise interventions and work with sex offenders, do so within this hegemony, basing their work within the values and understandings which stem from it. It is true to say that the way we understand a problem defines how we seek to solve it. Therefore, our culture and how we see our place within it necessarily define our interventions. The theories, which underpin developments in practice, have also been formulated within this dominant value system. At the same time, workers and offenders have developed their own sexual identities, their own place within this culture, as insiders or outsiders. The dominant value system impacts on all of us differently depending on our gender, sexual orientation, sexual life histories and life experiences, our degree of security within our own identity and how much that identity exists as part of the heterosexist, macho, hegemony, or exists despite it.

Probation staff are rarely given the opportunity to understand their work and what it does to them in this context. As a result, they are left to find personal survival mechanisms, when it is the responsibility of the organisation that demands their intervention, to devise a structure and strategy which integrates values, practice, support, supervision, training and counselling. In the latter section we will go on to examine the impact of the work on us as workers.

The Public Reaction: The Cultural Context Laid Bare

Sexual offences against children of either sex, and to a lesser extent, against adult women have attracted a huge amount of media interest in the past decade. The 'public' has a reported view of sex offending, and offenders, which is driven by news headlines, dramas, documentaries etc., which contain details designed to elicit voyeuristic responses, wrapped in outraged decency. Governments and legislators respond to these moral panics by crisis intervention: passing laws, which seem to be piecemeal responses to perceived threats.

High profile cases of sex offenders released from prison have led to laws designed to fill loopholes left by previous legislation.

This activity creates more panic reaction; underlying it is the belief that sex offending lies outside the experience of most normal people: it is perpetrated by monsters whose values, attitudes and reasoning are unrecognisable. The fact is that 80 per cent of sexual abuse or offending against children is perpetrated in either the victim's or the offender's home, by an adult in a position of trust. Stranger abuse, when the child does not know the offender, accounts for only 20 per cent (Grubin, 1999). Nevertheless, most newspaper column inches, community uproar, hatred and violence are directed to the high profile sex offender who comes out of gaol. The characteristics of his offending become the mark of 'the sex offender', leading to vigilante groups, housing bans, community notifications and public vilification.

The notions of protection of children and protection of self become confused; and concentrating upon the extreme cases takes away resources and energy from tackling the reality of abuse by known adults. But at the same time it allows people to define themselves as decent, representing all that is the opposite of a sex offender. This confusion, with its false understandings of sex offending, leads to the expectation that abuse can be stopped by more and more draconian legislation. The agencies dealing with the offenders: the police, probation and health and social services are served with these expectations and when the abuse and damage does not stop, the agencies are blamed.

Sex offending must be seen in cultural terms, as a consequence of the way we think and behave. Otherwise it will continue to be understood as the behaviour of others, instead of behaviour which is at one end of a spectrum of sexual activity, the legality and acceptability of which is culturally defined.

Working Within the Context

Probation officers who work on an every day basis with sex offenders are thus confronted with behaviour that strikes at our inner selves: we are sexual beings dealing with sexual behaviour that is abusive. It is behaviour that is an abuse of power, unwanted, and violent. It is frequently an abuse of the trust that children have in adults, by the nature of a particular relationship, or simply because of the status and power that children lack. It is behaviour that results from the beliefs and attitudes, the 'distorted cognitions', that sex offenders hold towards others, and in particular towards women and children.

Understanding sex offending in this way, rather than as inexplicable behaviour perpetrated by a few 'beasts' with uncontrolled libidos, has consequences for us as workers. Offences stem from attitudes and beliefs that are commonly shared within a male dominated hegemony, but which in the case of sex offenders, allow them to commit humiliating, violent, abusive acts against others. The victims and survivors of these acts are overcome by threats, guilt, self-blame or persuasion that they deserve it; by physical restraint, emotional threats or pretence that this is normal behaviour between people who 'love' each other. None of these mechanisms to overcome a victim are unfamiliar within sexual relationships, so that when we are confronted by sex offending, we are confronted by a part of our selves. This is why the work is so demanding, and why it can so damage individuals if the nature of the work is not understood, recognised and supported by the organisation.

The probation service has been working with adult male sex offenders for the past two decades. Our aim has been to reduce the risk of re-offending and to prevent further abuse. Within the context described above it is important to define the terms we use:

Sex offenders: our experience in the main has been to work with men who have been convicted of one or more sexually violent offence. Studies show (Abel *et al.*, 1987) that the prevalence of sexually abusive behaviour and oppression is far greater than the number of recorded offences and convictions. 'Self-report' studies record an alarming number of offences owned by men who have been given the assurance of confidentiality, and consequently the immunity from prosecution.

Sex offences: these are legally defined pieces of behaviour that our society defines as unacceptable and liable to legal sanctions.

Our therapeutic interventions are naturally determined by these legal definitions but in addition they are underpinned by our values and understandings. These values are culturally relative, in that they stemmed from a particular feminist perspective which has been 'fine tuned' by experience, research and a developing theoretical base. We understand sex offending as behaviour which men can control and take responsibility for, that it is harmful, whatever amount of physical or psychological violence is used and that sex offending, whoever perpetrates it, is an abuse of power.

These have not always been the pervading truths and values: for many workers, as much as offenders, they were difficult to own. Some workers, like some sentencers, may never be able to do so. As the values in our society jostle for pre-eminence, this inevitably has an impact on how we view the motivation of those who offend against those values, and thus on our interventions with offenders.

Cutural Dilemmas

The fact that we cannot understand, or work, outside our culture or our value laden legal structure is clearly illustrated with a couple of dilemmas currently facing probation staff on a day to day basis:

1. *The 'Age of Consent' debate.* Currently the legal age for homosexual men to engage in consensual sexual activity is below that for heterosexual men. There are also legal constraints about such behaviour which do not apply to heterosexual acts. In this debate, there exists an institutionalised heterosexism, disguised as a series of moral confusions, which contribute to homophobia. One is the understandable desire to protect young people. However, in the main young men are sexually active with other young men, in their late teens and early twenties.

Another is the desire to regulate sexual activity of any sort because the proliferation of sexual activity breeds disease and the breakdown of the moral order (Christian heterosexual marriage, which is necessary to sustain the status quo for the most powerful). However, heterosexuals can marry at

16 years and young women and girls in Britain are engaging in sexual intercourse, becoming pregnant and having babies at a faster rate than other European countries.

Thirdly there is the propagation of the view that all gay men (unlike heterosexual men!) are indiscriminate and predatory in their sexual behaviour, and will thus prey on unsuspecting or unaware 16 or 17-year-old young men. Finally there is the confusion, deliberately fostered out of ignorance and prejudice, between homosexuality and paedophilia.

How do probation officers prepare court reports on young men of 16 to 17 years who are convicted for an activity which would be consensual if they were heterosexual? How can we suggest how the 'offending behaviour' should be tackled? How should we prepare plans to prevent 're-offending' if the court makes a community order and expects such activity of us?

2. Legislative attitudes and laws in relation to women. Legislation relating to offences against women and comments by the judiciary in passing sentence on men convicted of offences against women enshrine attitudes that militate against the workers' values and treatment objectives.

Firstly, in passing sentence, members of the judiciary (of whom the vast majority are white, public school educated men of undisclosed sexuality) have provided offenders with strong re-enforcement of their attitudes, justifications and denials. This is powerfully done by passing blame onto the victim or minimising the harm experienced. The judges' comments are remembered, used and regurgitated word for word by entrenched offenders.

In some instances, sentencers will collude with the distorted belief that a man's sexual needs are uncontrollable, and that women know this and therefore should not provoke his 'natural' inclination i.e. women can contribute to an offence or even cause it. Phrases like 'contributory negligence' have been used in open court to describe victim's behaviour in cases of rape.

The phrase 'she was asking for it', is often used by offenders to justify their actions, and the same unspoken belief can be abstracted from some sentencers' comments on the reason for the shortness of the custodial sentence they have just passed.

Thirdly, until recently the offence of rape was not recognised within marriage. This situation enshrined all of those attitudes of subjugation, ownership of mind, body and soul, of control and a woman's loss of self-control over her destiny.

Cultural Relevance

Without a stated understanding of how the cultural relevance of legislation impacts on our work, and us, we cannot take into account our own sense of self and sexual identity, those of the offenders, and the interaction of the two.

We may indeed be working in ways that oppress those offenders, and workers, whose sense of identity has been developed in contradiction to the heterosexist imperative and the particularly 'macho' brand of masculinity which dominates British culture.

Sex offences, and the attitudes and behaviours of offenders need to be seen through the following cultural prism:

Our state, and the institutions which support it, are fundamentally racist, sexist and heterosexist i.e. our laws, codes of behaviour, liberties and rights favour the white, male heterosexual.

Masculinity of the 'real men should behave like men' variety, acts as a yardstick against which all men's behaviour and their sexual activity is defined.

Individual life and sexual histories have been developed within this culture, and behaviour should be interpreted through it, and not through an ideal world of the worker's own devising.

'Acceptable' and 'unacceptable' ways of thinking of, and behaving towards, women and children are part of our cultural spectrum. Men can be placed along it. Men think in acceptable/non acceptable ways to a greater or lesser degree. If workers fail to grasp this concept, then they are in danger of making the mistake of looking at sex offenders as 'a thing apart'.

Literature and research indicate that sex offenders, men who never get convicted, and those who occupy the 'law abiding' group differ little in their attitudes, beliefs or arousal patterns (Malamuth, 1981; Muelenhard and Linton, 1987; Rappaport and Burkhart, 1984). In essence women workers must remember that their male colleague workers and those whom they seek to treat, may differ only marginally in any of these respects and plan their survival accordingly.

Vilification and abuse have always been used by those in power, or fearful of losing their power, to avoid any investigation of their own realities and to define themselves in stark contrast. The creation of the sex offender as a beast is powerfully used by our institutions (the public, media, politicians, care and criminal justice agencies) to engender fear and set the offender and their behaviour outside normality.

Workers engaged in work with sex offenders must continually raise these issues presented by a dominant heterosexist culture; a culture/society which has a particular view of masculinity and of the place of women and children in it, and which is still fundamentally a racist society. The interplay of different oppressions in the life experiences and sexual histories of the workers and offenders has a primary importance when we are working with sexual violence. The articulation of these issues and their incorporation in programmes of work has, as yet, not even been attempted systematically. The problem we then pose for ourselves is, working as we do without articulating our context, we may be attempting to impose a reality on the offender and ourselves. We are requiring sex offenders to adopt an OK version of the heterosexist male, in a world dominated by a masculinity against which they cannot measure up, nor perhaps want to, according to their own sense of self.

The Impact of the Work

Within this cultural relativity, our current understanding of sex offending informs the way we seek to intervene. If we do not accept prevailing male ideologies but instead believe that men are responsible for their behaviour and can control it, then we need to work on the denials that are used by sex offenders to excuse or justify that behaviour. The denials are of responsibility, harm, self-control, and the denial of the victim experience.

In order to break down these denials, which are made up of attitudes and beliefs, much of the work has been based in a cognitive behavioural approach. This approach involves enabling offenders to identify errors in their thinking (denials) which have allowed them to commit offences. It challenges an offender's way of thinking and enables them to learn and adopt strategies to prevent them relapsing into previous thinking errors and consequent offending patterns.

Fundamentally, it means that we, the workers are engaged in a long hard struggle to challenge long held, entrenched attitudes and beliefs. These are not so very different to generally held attitudes, and are essential to disinhibition and then abuse.

It can feel that the difference between offenders and the rest of the male population is only a matter of degree. This feeling engenders others for each worker, depending on their gender, sexuality, and life history.

The cognitive behavioural approach to assessment and therapy challenges notions of male socialisation; of masculinity linked to dominance; coercion and performance; male sexual aggression as a logical extension of the male role and heterosexual sex and as the socially acceptable expression of masculinity. Our work depends on acquiring detailed descriptions of sexual violence through assumptive questioning. These accounts of behaviours and the thoughts and feelings that led up to them are essential, to the assessments of motivation and risk which inform the nature of the work we then undertake.

It is not difficult to understand that using cognitive behavioural theory and methods will have an impact on workers. It is worth reminding ourselves that it is the nature of the offending that makes the work so stressful.

The work exposes us to powerful emotions and distorted accounts of violent and abusive behaviour. Not only do we listen, within an intense officer-client relationship, to distorted notions of sexuality, sexual development, power and blame, but the material is intensely distressing. Probation officers do not have the option of choice of which clients will be our responsibility. We work with all sex offenders, those who abuse children or adults; those sentenced to community and custodial sentences and at all stages of the criminal justice process. How much work we are able to do with each offender will depend on several variables, however we cannot refuse to accept what we are statutorily obliged to accept. The impact on us of the material that we have to absorb is undeniable.

It is in the nature of the probation service to focus all our energies and resources on the impact we can have on the perpetrator, in our efforts to make them 'safer' people: our purpose being to protect the public. What often gets lost or sidelined, then, is any real examination of how the nature of the work impacts on the worker. In this next section we consider this impact and its consequences.

If we feel optimistic that a good quality, consistent, professionally delivered and researched programme is going to bring about a shift in attitude and ultimately a change in behaviour, why is so little attention paid to a systematic and thorough support service for the team of workers delivering it? Whilst we value our contribution to the work, and believe that our intervention is right and appropriate, how much thought is given to the personal cost of our contribution?

The Personal Cost

The cost can be perceived and experienced in a number of ways. It can be counted in a certain loss of objective observation of the everyday activities of families, lone men, children at play, even our relatives and friends. We lose the facility often, to trust that what we see is what is really happening, and that there is no 'ulterior motive' in an adult's caring behaviour and no sexual motivation in ordinary pursuits of adults with children. We sometimes lose the ability to trust, we have to guard against suspicion, over protection of our own children and cynicism: all of which impact also on our families and closest friends, our partners and our colleagues.

We can be sitting in a cafeteria on a Saturday morning, watching a man wrap a child up against the cold outside, and instead of seeing a caring father we imagine the whole behaviour as inappropriate touching, an elaborate charade and an excuse to fondle the child. We can catch sight of someone watching a group of boys playing football in the park, and see them as engaging in masturbatory fantasies, or targeting a vulnerable child. Suddenly we realise that former images have lost their innocence by becoming acts that could be interpreted as sexually inappropriate.

Alongside the suspicions and interpretations, are the emotional reactions we begin to have to simple images of children and babies being cared for lovingly. Every day at work we are learning that so many small children have never experienced that love and concern, or have only been cared for in return for their silence and compliance.

When we are working exclusively with sex offenders, as we do on the Sex Offender Treatment Programmes in prison, or in teams in the community which specialise in sex offender work, the consequences are greater. We feel that our 'warped' view of the world and our concerns, our fears for ourselves and how we think, can only be safely shared between ourselves. Our families may find our suspicious turn of mind uncomfortable to live with, and they certainly would not wish often to hear about our day's work.

At the same time our thoughts and interpretations of the world can threaten to overwhelm us. We cannot stop them outside work, and at work they correspond with the intimate and graphic details of a sex offender's abusive behaviour. This presents us with the dilemma of how to cope with these feelings of disgust and anger on the one hand, and how to present ourselves in a professional and enabling manner on the other. This dilemma, and the feelings that engender it, should be openly recognised and a resolution sought for individual workers through structured and well resourced counselling and supervision. We need to be able to keep a sense of equilibrium in this work and in our life outside the work in order to do it well, and to stay well ourselves.

The Cost to Sense of Self

Any work with sex offenders, whether in groups or individually, heightens our awareness of our own gender and sexuality. The vast proportion of sex offenders we deal with are male and the majority of their victims are either female (adult and child) or male children. In a groupwork situation it is quite common to be the only female in the room. We become aware of our physical appearance, height, weight, age and our femaleness. This heightens our sense of isolation within the group and our awareness of our 'otherness' both inside and outside that group. If the group is being run in a prison setting that sense of isolation may be further reinforced by a predominantly male staff group in the wider work setting. These responses have an immediacy about them, but there are other issues which may not surface until a later stage. What happens to our own sexuality, attitudes and behaviour?

Listening to sex offenders can trigger thought processes, which may have been buried in our own sexual history. For some workers, what they hear is a repeat of their own experience of abuse, or what a close member of their family had to endure. It may be that they recognise patterns of behaviour from their own lives, or the perpetrator's victim has the same name as their own, or their partner, or their child.

The work can also lead us to examine our own sexual relationships and orientation. Sexual fantasies usually remain private and hidden behind closed doors. The courage of the victim's disclosure, more often than not will not lead to a conviction. When it does, any treatment programme exposes a hidden world of secrecy, distortion, sexual gratification and pain.

What do we as Workers Think and Feel When we Unlock this Hidden World?

From our own experience, and in talking and working with other women workers, there is an anger and revulsion, directed against men in general, and sex offenders specifically. We may find ourselves viewing all men as sex offenders, as men's behaviour towards us mirrors the offenders' behaviour, but the mirror is distorted and warped. If the aim of our work is to reduce risk through encouraging offenders to accept responsibility and change their behaviour, we have to challenge these distorted thoughts and behaviours. This is demanding work; it promotes an often conflictual environment which by its very nature impacts on the worker.

There is the danger that our anxieties will spill over into our personal and private lives. We begin to examine what dangers our children and grandchildren are exposed to. We can become over protective as we warn our families and friends about the dangers of normal social intercourse; taken too far we begin to put our children at risk by never allowing them to be exposed to the possibility of having to take action to protect themselves. Our world can become a world full of sex offenders.

We feel, as workers, responsible for the protection of the vulnerable in society. There is a difficult balance to hold here. In our work, we concentrate on getting the sex offender to take responsibility for their offending and any future behaviour, and work hard to shift the responsibility from the victim, on whom it is so often imposed by offender and society alike, onto the offender. Outside the work we can often fail to protect ourselves from assuming the blame when men re-offend. This sense of helplessness becomes intensified by each tabloid press headline announcing in detail the exploits of the latest paedophile ring or serial rapist. We know that therapy is not a cure, but the beginning in a long journey of self discovery. The only person who is ultimately responsible for breaking the offending pattern is the perpetrator. However, this does not stop us internalising what we see as our own personal failure whenever a person repeats their offence.

Women workers can feel particularly threatened by stereotypical attitudes commonly held by men and by male sex offenders to allow them to do what they want to women and children. Women 'ask for it', are 'bitches', 'slappers' and 'tarts'. Children should 'do as they are told', 'need to be shown', or 'deserve punishment'. All these beliefs endorse and justify abusive behaviour and give permission for the offending to continue.

Perpetrators will often sexualise their comments and try to assume power and control over the female worker by making them feel and appear stupid. They can recognise how uncomfortable we can sometimes feel, and highlight and exploit that discomfort. Some men are adept at making us feel soiled and degraded by describing their offences in graphic terms, using derogatory words and phrases for sexual actions and female genitalia. Other men change their behaviour in the opposite direction, and deliberately avoid using crude terminology, or avoid swearing. The presence of a 'lady' in the room seems to alter their accounts of their behaviour, either because they appear embarrassed, or think that we would 'not want to hear that sort of thing'. The same self-censorship and rectitude does not apply to the carrying out of the behaviour itself!

Female workers use different responses to this maleness and it is important that the approach is 'thought out' rather than instinctual. Some workers for example have found themselves in turn adopting a masculine approach in an attempt to 'belong' or to be accepted into the group or to distance ourselves from their stereotypes. There is also the issue of language to be used. What becomes acceptable within the group dynamics may be totally unacceptable to us in our 'outside world'. Certainly the topic areas which we spend all day analysing may not be acceptable for use in our private lives.

A crucial relationship within the treatment framework is the one that exists between the workers, and we usually try to work within a male/female pairing. A gender balance is considered ideal, and we work hard to ensure this balance; practice suggests that we do not consider the balance of different sexual orientation in worker pairings to be either as relevant or as simple to recruit. Whatever our sexual orientation, however, it is vital for female workers to feel supported by their male colleagues, indeed, we expect male colleagues to take the lead role in challenging sexism within the treatment group. If our male colleagues share the attitudes and aspects of masculinity which support the stereotypes used by the offenders, then not only are they less effective, but they are potentially damaging to the progress of the offender, and the self image and confidence of their female colleagues.

In our experience, our male colleagues often feel immense guilt on behalf of their own gender as a consequence of being involved in this work. The true impact of the work on men within their personal lives, and how the material with which they engage affects how they conduct their own relationships should be explored. The supervision and support of our male colleagues are essential to preserve a sense of balance, their emotional health and that of their families. Male workers for instance sometimes stop taking on the caring role and tasks with their children that they have hitherto undertaken without thinking, such as bathing them or taking them swimming. Such activities put them in an intimate, and wholly appropriate relationship to their children. But this is one that they know only too well could be misconstrued, or interpreted differently, since they spend their working days interpreting the behaviour of sex offenders in just such activity. Some of our male colleagues experience extreme sexual dysfunction as a result of the work, such as loss of libido, or impotence; sometimes their relationships end, or they are marginalised by colleagues either because of a sense of contamination or because their awareness is too painful for those colleagues to share.

Survival

The work can thus affect our sense of self worth and our self image. It can lead to sexual and emotional dysfunction, self loathing and an antipathy towards the other gender. It can harm our relationships with each other and with partners and families.

In order to survive the experience, formal coping and supportive mechanisms should be in place. These are dealt with towards the end of the chapter. However, to conclude this section on the impact of the work on the workers we need to point to the equally important development of informal coping strategies. Inevitably we develop a close affinity to our colleague workers, a very thick skin, a shockingly macabre sense of humour and a desensitisation to the use of words that most of us do not use with people with whom we are not on intimate terms! These attributes are essential to our own survival within this work.

What is the Point of all this Work?

What response do we expect from those who are on the receiving end of our interventions? It is important to remember that for some of them, their conviction and possible exclusion from society is just a mild irritant that prevents them temporarily from re-offending. Some indeed go on trying to maintain their influence over actual and potential victims from their prison cells through letters, phone calls and visits, and prison staff have to be eternally vigilant monitors.

How do we stop men from being sexually attracted to children, or aroused by perpetrating degrading and humiliating acts on women?

The simple answer is that we don't.

What we can do is to heighten their awareness of the warning signs, the rehearsals and the deliberate seeking out of situations in which they can offend. It is essential to provide offenders with a powerful victim image, one that will help to deter them from seeking out their next victim. They are helped to develop coping skills, and strategies to use in future risky situations.

Good practice dictates that we should target offenders appropriately, as haphazard selection and intervention can do more harm than good. Programmes of work with these men should be long-term, focused, consistent and presented by trained and motivated staff. Clear learning aims and objectives should be identified and an individual's progress monitored. Throughout our intervention, an offenders risk must be assessed and re-assessed. Whatever work is undertaken by men in prison should be continued in the community to prevent relapse into their offending pattern and this involves considerable liaison between prison and probation services.

Realistically, of course, once an offender's period of statutory supervision has terminated, he is left to fend for himself. Only the individual's motivation not to re-offend will help him return to the coping strategies learnt during treatment. The unpalatable truth for society is that we are not talking about a precise science. There is no such thing as 'nil risk' and the legislators, public and media must face up to this. There are no magic formulae, or overnight cures.

For those of us who have the responsibility to minimise the risks presented by these offenders, and who hear every day the detailed descriptions of what men are capable of inflicting on others less powerful than themselves, there is the danger that we take on the responsibility for the behaviour, because we too want to believe that we can work miraculous change.

The Future Direction

In order for workers to make sense of this work, do it well and survive, the following measures should be in place:

- Workers should have counselling provided on a regular basis, by an outside, appropriate agency. This facility will promote objectivity, engender confidence and offer a safe and supportive environment to off load and re-energise.
- The provision of regular in-house supervision is essential. This would ensure that responsibility for the work is located within the service providing it. It would also maintain accountability of professional practice within the organisation and inform management of the quality of the service provision.

- Support systems and networks should be set up and maintained amongst the workers. This would decrease stress levels, diminish the sense of isolation felt by individuals and reduce the negative impact of the work which we all experience to different degrees, at different times.
- Adequate and ongoing training should be in place in order to keep workers informed about research findings, new methods of work and research based approach to practice. Regular training should also address issues of competence, professionalism, standards of practice, and provide an additional support network for staff engaged in this work.
- Adequate resources should be made available for workers to develop programmes that address concepts of patriarchy and issues of male domination, and material that is equally relevant to heterosexual and homosexual participants.
- Resources should be available to ensure the development of culturally relevant material. Training should involve the exploration of cultural diversity and the impact of this within a culturally diverse group of both offenders and practitioners.
- More management strategies should be developed in order to ensure the 'safety' aspect of the practitioner's situation is taken into consideration. This could ensure that early signs of stress are recognised and addressed, and would not ignore the different stresses involved for different staff.
- There must be an acceptance at a national level that best practice can only be assured when resources, training, and programme development and evaluation are not left to local exigencies.

Conclusion

This chapter may have gone some way to widen the debate about the cost to each one of us, and to our society, of the way we allow ourselves to behave towards each other.

The victim experience makes banner headlines. The impact of the abuser on them is acknowledged. The impact of the work on those who aim to prevent further victimisation is less well understood. Unless the measures we have pointed to, are taken account of by those who expect us to do the work, there will be casualties.

References

Abel, C.G., Becker, J.B. *et al.* (1987) Self Reported Sex Crimes of Non-Incarcerated Paedophilliacs. *Journal of Interpersonal Violence.* (1): pp3–25.

Grubin, D. (1999) Sex Offending against Children: Understanding the Risk. Executive Summary (p v) *Police Research Papers*: London, Home Office Publications.

Home Office, (1998) *HM Inspectorate of Probation Report of Thematic Inspection Exercising Constant Vigilance. The Role of the Probation Service in Protecting the Public from Sex Offenders.* London, Home Office Publications.

Malamuth, N.M. (1981) Rape Proclivity Among Males. *Journal of Social Issues.* 37: pp138–157.

Muelenhard, C.L. and Linton, M.A. (1987) Date Rape and Sexual Aggression in Dating Situations: Incidence and Risk Factors. *Journal of Counselling Psychology.* 34: pp186–196.

Rappaport, K. and Burkhart, B.R. (1984) Personality and Attitudinal Characteristics of Sexually Coercive College Males. *Journal; Of Abnormal Psychology.* 93: pp216–221.

CHAPTER 4

Racism is Catching

Clarence Allen

Racism is catching. It affects us without us even being aware that it has impacted on our lives.

This was a comment that I overheard at a discussion group for black young people that I was co-facilitating. When it became clear that the majority of the group did not understand what the statement was meant to convey, the participant explained that he had gone into a shop to purchase a present. Not wanting to be seen to be doing anything untoward, he picked up any items he wanted to see with his sleeves metaphorically rolled up and his hands in full view of the security men. He went on to explain that he was not aware that he had done this until he had left the shop and his friend pointed out that he looked very uncomfortable. With some degree of self-disgust he remembered what had happened.

The group echoed this initial comment and was able to relate similar stories about how racism subconsciously affected their lives. Men crossed over streets to avoid walking behind white women. Hands were taken out of pockets to show that they were not concealing weapons. Hearts raced when passing policemen despite innocence.

Similarly homophobia and heterosexism are infectious. The result, it seems, remains so powerful that children still bandy around insults about lesbians and gay men, without truly knowing their meaning or implication, and get into fights because someone accused them of not being heterosexual. References to lesbians and gay men are uttered in hushed tones around children who then, inaccurately, understand them to be dirty and evil.

A training session in which I posed the question about things that the group were told about lesbians and gay men when they were younger received answers ranging from nothing at all through to vehemently homophobic comments or television programmes being switched over or off. Adults seemed reluctant to talk about (homo) sexuality in front of the children.

The BBC2 television documentary, *Sleeping with the Enemy*, put together two heterosexual men with two gay men. The former pair, who were at pains to let the world know they were one hundred per cent heterosexual, were insulted beyond belief that someone could think they were gay. The thought alone was such anathema to them that they could not simply let the mistake go unchallenged and uncorrected. Despite being sure of their sexuality and apparently comfortable with it, the possibility that others believed they were not 'normal' overrode all sense of logic and reason. They were unable to see that the effect of their homophobia was more powerful and longer lasting than the false assumptions about their sexuality.

Surely being falsely assumed to be gay is not tantamount to having to address the impact of homophobia and heterosexism on lesbians and gay men. Similarly a white person gets affronted if they are accused of racism. Their defences rise to protect their innocence but this merely acts as a smokescreen to hide the issue at hand. When women accuse me of being sexist, my first reaction, if I remain ignorant of my actions, is not to say I am not, nor could ever be, sexist, as I have many friends who are women! My reaction is to ask what I have done to receive the initial comment. It is only then can I think about the implications and, if I feel it valid, then I change my views/actions. If I do not accept the explanation I have every right to challenge it, just as the person has every right to make the comment. It is a two-way learning curve where both sides need to be open not only to logical answers but also to emotions and empathy. To endeavour to simplify it further: a child cannot simply be *told* that it is wrong to pull a cat's tail without it being explained to it about the pain the cat feels.

What I hope to do in this chapter is to highlight where these potent views around racism and homophobia originate before moving on to addressing racism and homophobia together.

Black men and women have been raised in a society that is undeniably racist. In spite of many changes and progressions, it cannot be denied that this statement, still, in the late nineties, remains the reality. It could also be argued that those who claim never to have experienced discrimination based on their race need to educate themselves about the diurnal actuality of their lives where stereotypes of black people abound.

Although the Race Relation Act and the Race Discrimination Act are in place to give official backing to challenge racism and grant some power to affect change and right injustices, overt racism continues to be rife. It is seen in graffiti in the streets, heard in chants on football terraces and from the windows of moving cars, experienced in the shop that caused the above-mentioned man to overplay his probity. There is the subtler, although not always so, more covert racism that is pervasive in most institutions: the police, the judicial system, adoption agencies, the employment field. Both overt and covert racism impact with differing degrees on the lives of black people. Both can often be the start for internalised racism, the racism that makes black men handle objects as a magician would or make black people think we should be grateful for the little we are given.

This was best typified for me during the 'sweet' exercise. In this session, similar to the stepping stone exercise, group participants are each given a different character scenario and asked to take a sweet if they were able, as their given character, to complete different tasks without much difficulty. The bowl of sweets included expensive Belgian chocolates, wrapped in gold-coloured paper, less exciting sweets and went down, in terms of taste, to the much loathed aniseed balls. What invariably happens is that the first sweets to go are the exciting ones with the least attractive ones left for last. Given that the tasks included getting a mortgage with a partner, adopting a child with your partner, being open about your sexuality when applying for jobs, feeling at ease entering an unknown pub alone, etc., those who had characters from traditionally disadvantaged groups ended up with the mangy sweets. Those who had the poorer sweets, instead of feeling it unfair that others had better sweets, were glad they had some at all. Indeed, this is true of life where disadvantaged groups feel grateful for poor quality housing, badly paid jobs or poor services, and are reluctant to complain for fear of reprisals. Black people have long been made to believe that we do not deserve better.

The society in which we find ourselves, fuelled by mis-representation in films, books, television, the news, advertising, tells us in many different ways that black people, and black men in particular, are a collection of some, if not all, of the following adjectives: strong, aggressive, threatening, loud, exotic, sexually both exciting and frightening, active, violent, criminal (drug suppliers, rapists, muggers), unintelligent, unemployable, anti-establishment and, quite conspicuously for this piece, heterosexual. It would not be difficult for even the most naive person to find copious examples that demonstrate this.

As a result, black people, especially men, find themselves facing a dichotomy. We are ostracised by a society that we have every right to want to make a claim on, yet we also want to distance ourselves from a society that so readily gives us a poor name.

Nevertheless, today, there exists an inconsistency where the social signifiers that have traditionally been used as shorthand for 'Black' have become buzzwords for 'cool'. The media uses 'Black' jargon to sell everything from soft drinks to perfumes. Popular culture and music is full of images and references that common sense thinking would perceive to be Black. The performer Madonna has based her success on the appropriation of Black sub-culture. Young people adopt styles, mannerisms and expressions that are traditionally viewed as Black. This wannabe culture became so obvious that the term 'wigger' (an amalgamation of 'white' and 'nigger') was coined. It has become almost acceptable to parody Blackness for the sake of style. While it may be chic to want to be Black, the negativity that exists towards *real* Black people still is very strong.

The legacy of racist stereotyping, no doubt stemming as far back as the periods of both colonialism and slavery, remains. It can be argued that from these times two still very popular stereotypes of Black men originate. Black men were perceived to be stronger than their white contemporaries, not based on any fair sporting competition, but because the crack of a leather whip was very effective tool to make muscles work. Good, strong Black male slaves, in a way not dissimilar to stud racehorses in stables, were made to father children to ensure healthy strong offsprings who, in turn, would be extra hands for the slave master. Black men were seen as animals, as a commodity, used to move heavy goods, toil hard land and impregnate Black women. Black men being viewed as bestial also legitimised the mistreatment doled out on plantations or slave ships.

Being physically strong or sexually potent are not particularly negative attributes. On the contrary they are characteristics most people, Black or white, gay or heterosexual, male or female, would view as positive and desirable. These characteristics become problematic when the aforementioned coupling of strength and sexual prowess exist in isolation of other positive attributes, such as sensitivity, creativity, understanding and co-operation, which traditionally had been discouraged or crushed in slaves.

Slaves were very rarely taught to read or write, thus stifling any capacity for greater learning and building on intelligence. Creativity of expression was discouraged; so much of this creativity went underground. Black men were only allowed to be physically strong and priapic and this was controlled by the slave owners. Black women were viewed as child bearers and rearers without any intellect or seen as sexual objects for the pleasure of the slave owners.

While the actual metal chains have gone, it seems that very little has changed today. Black men I work with still make comments that, when at school, they were pushed into sport and actively encouraged to do 'manual' studies as opposed to concentrating on the academic. The Black women had to push to be taken seriously in their studies.

The media, television and film in particular, uses a stereotypical view of Black people and perpetuate myths surrounding strength, sexuality and sexual prowess. There have been very few depictions of rounded Black characters, and most of them are extremely recent. The cult film director Quentin Tarantino has been criticised by his contemporary Spike Lee for his depictions of Black men, for reinforcing stereotypes whether perceived to be positive or negative. However, it was only recently, in *Get On The Bus,* that Lee introduced his first male character that was neither heterosexual nor stereotypically gay.

Given that so very few positive attributes are offered to Black men it is understandable that we should claim, and want to keep, the two that are on offer to us. Black men embrace this myth of increased sexual stamina and performance and use it to their advantage. The men in the Black-only discussion group said that they played up their sexual ability and, to varying degrees, pandered to the stereotype to secure sexual partners. They also claimed to use the fallacy that they are strong to deter possible confrontational situations. I would doubt that Francis Cress Wellsing had fight minimisation in mind when he wrote, 'Black people are the most feared people in the world.' Yet the Black men in this group saw using stereotypes to their advantage as a means to an end.

Unfortunately the stereotypical, and undeniably racist, conception of what it means to be Black is restrictive. Essentially this view of being Black becomes definitive as opposed to descriptive. By this, it can be argued that Black ought to describe either race or ethnic make-up and should not be a by-word for characteristics or qualities. Unfortunately for many of the men in the group the term Black *was* definitive. Sadly, more often than not, this definition was one they believed they had thoughtfully formulated, but is a re-interpretation of white perceptions of Blackness, thus internalising the oppression. If they considered that they fell outside of this definition, which is not of their own making, their Blackness was open to question and/or reduced.

This raises questions of assimilation and integration, which are invariably seen as 'selling out' or 'opting in' respectively. Neither was seen to be particularly appealing. It was for some a no-win situation where to succeed in our society some personal integrity had to be compromised. Black men that were seen to be successful were also considered to have compromised their Blackness and Black identity. Men such as Frank Bruno, Andi Peters and Linford Christie were viewed as poor role models for a generation raised under the spectre of racism, based on their either being effeminate (Peters) or their appropriation of the Union Jack flag (Christie), for many an act of treason against the Black community.

Given that there are so few role models for Black people, it falls upon the few that are in a position to affect change to be the panacea. What happens is that these role models are set up to fail. Alternatively we become critical of those, due to our own internalised racism, that we do not perceive to be Black enough. As a result so called good role models perpetuate myths about Black men or pander to traditional stereotypes. As a rule, Eddie Murphy and Wil Smith both play very two-dimensional characters in films. Though to be fair Smith did attempt to play a homosexual con artiste in *Six Degrees of Separation*, albeit without the gumption or conviction of Adrian Lester on stage. The actress Cathy Tyson seems forever to be cast as a prostitute. It is very telling that Melanie B, the Black woman in the Spice Girls, with a pierced tongue and dressed in animal prints, is labelled 'scary'.

At a press conference during the well-documented criminal case against Mike Tyson when he was accused of raping a woman, Louis Farrakhan, the powerful leader of the Nation of Islam, made some comments. These were more or less equal to justifying the violation, claiming that if she willingly went into a room with a man like Mike, and it was implied a hot-blooded heterosexual man, she knew what to expect. The alarming truth was these comments were not challenged by anyone on the panel, but laughed about knowingly.

Here was a perfect example of Black men themselves perpetuating the myth of a Black man being a predatory sexual animal. While Mike Tyson has positive attributes that might make him a good role model, it is sad that it is the negative that affords him kudos.

In a way not dissimilar to the term Black being seen as definitive, the term gay has also taken on definitive connotations and qualities. The gay community is itself guilty of creating limiting views of gayness with seemingly interchangeable and cloned clubs, periodicals, fashions and styles that define how gay someone is. This does not allow for much individuality or personal freedom of expression. At least, not without a struggle.

Despite homophobia and racism being two very separate ills, they have similarities in that they both have the capacity to cause great pain, can both operate overtly and covertly and can both be institutionalised and internalised.

A member of a lesbian and gay group I facilitated said that the only difference between the oppressions of racism and homophobia is that it is not necessary to have to come out as being Black. While this comment proved to be a simplistic approach to multiple discrimination, it nevertheless highlighted some of the issues around sexuality and generated a discussion about the equality of all oppressions. I strongly believe that no oppression is worse than another. The effects on the person or persons who find themselves on the receiving end of any oppression are unquestionably painful and potentially damaging. Thus to endeavour to create a hierarchy of oppressions allows people to opt out of challenging all discrimination. It gives permission to focus solely upon one oppression and, consequentially, sanctions the neglecting of what is felt to be a lesser oppression. This is more often than not a selfish or lazy excuse to justify a reluctance to tackle oppressions that do not directly affect our personal lives.

While co-running a training session on sexuality with a number of Black probation officers in London the session was highjacked by a section who were adamant that homophobia was not as terrible as racism. Following conversations the group reasoned that it was easy for lesbians and gay men to hide their sexuality and that there was always the choice if people came out. It followed, their argument continued, that the effects of coming out were always a calculated risk. With regards to issues of race there was never a question of choice.

My co-trainer asked these dissenters if, given a choice, they would deny that they were Black if they could get away with it, say over the phone, and if it meant that they would not experience prejudice. There was a resounding negative response. The group based their answers on wanting to maintain some sense of integrity in their lives and not feeling able to live with the dishonesty. It was this revelation that allowed us to restart the session of sexuality properly, allowing us to point out that lesbians and gay men also possessed the quality of integrity. So, while it may sometimes be wise and, to be fair, possible to hide ones homosexuality, many do not. Besides, there are mechanisms, arguably ineffective, to challenge discrimination on grounds of race, but the mechanisms are there. The law does not have any recourse to counter discrimination against lesbians and gay men.

The very stereotypical images of lesbians and gay men were so powerful that the legacy still remains now. Gay men were, and to a degree still are, portrayed as the camp, flamboyant, effeminate, weak, misogynist and paedophilic originators of AIDS. Lesbians, until very recently with the advent of lesbian chic, were seen as highly political, butch, man-hating, shorthaired dungaree wearers. Stereotypes of both lesbians and gay men are ostensibly white.

In the media, films such as *Like It Is*, *My Best Friend's Wedding*, and *Priscilla, Queen of the Desert* and television programmes such as *Eastenders* and *This Life*, have all made moves to show much more rounded and complete, even if not totally likeable, lesbian and gay characters. It did not surprise me that Marlon Rigg's *Tongues Untied*, a short film about some of the issues faced by Black gay men, or Pratibha Parmar's *Khush*, (about the experiences of Asian lesbians and gay men) were both given television screenings well after the watershed. These portrayals are a long way away from the parodies of *Are You Being Served?* and *La Cage aux Folles*. Nevertheless, it should be noted that these portrayals served a purpose and are still to this day seen as groundbreaking.

Unquestionably there have been a significant developments that certain sections of the diverse lesbian and gay community have initiated. There have been campaigns to force the government to reduce the age of sexual consent for gay men from eighteen to sixteen. The annual Lesbian and Gay Pride Festival in London has seen its numbers grow higher and higher. There has been, born from the minds of several astute entrepreneurs, whether gay or not, the creation of self-professed gay ghettos in London, Manchester and Birmingham. These areas have proved to be very successful, so successful in fact that they have managed to create a different gay stereotype (albeit created by gay men themselves).

In a lesbian and gay group that I was co-facilitating a discussion was held about whether it is possible for a stereotype to be positive. The group was asked to identify stereotypes of lesbians and gay men that were prevalent when they were growing up and stereotypes of gay people today. The group felt that images of homosexuality portrayed by Larry Grayson and the characters played by Benny Hill or Dick Emery did not reflect their lives or experiences. Having gay feelings, it was felt, did not mean they were like these parodies and the group was quick to reject them outright. The group was equally eager to voice that it also did not identify with the cappuccino-drinking, tattooed, lycra-wearing, body-beautiful people of London's Soho or Manchester's Village, which it felt was an equally restrictive portrayal of gayness. The group saw these stereotypes as negative. When both facilitators asked the group to ignore whether they were positive or negative but whether these stereotypes were merely true we got a different response. Many of the group admitted to being camp or camping it up. Others admitted to spending evenings on pub-crawls on Old Compton Street ending up in Compton's café for bagels and a cup of espresso.

While running a session on stereotypes of Black sexuality, my opening exercise was to ask the group to answer ten questions about me, including, amongst others, where I lived, what was my favourite food, what type of car I drove. It was interesting that no one in the group, including the Black participants, assumed that my favourite food was rice and peas. I challenged the group about censorship and most admitted that they had feared being stereotypical. We all make assumptions based on stereotypes, this is inevitable, it is human nature, it is a measure for protection. From time to time these assumptions may be proven true. Assumptions for me are problematic when they are not checked out, when they prevent us from doing something. So while it is true that I am a Black man who enjoys rice and peas, I clearly do not eat them all the time!

Clearly some gay men are camp. Some Black men are muggers and rapists. Even thieves have other aspects to their personalities. Stereotypes can be true, but are only true of some people some of the time.

Nevertheless, in spite of the developments made by the lesbian and gay community, the original negative stereotypes of lesbians and gay men remain. It needs to be noted that of the list of stereotypes about lesbians and gay men above, only misogyny and paedophilia are problematic. It would be confining to condemn any man for being effeminate or camp or a woman for being butch or having short hair. However, for someone coming to terms with their lesbianism or homosexuality, the negativity surrounding either needs to be faced, addressed, challenged, then rejected, before any real positive progression can be made. For gay men the original reactions to the appearance of AIDS caused widespread homophobia.

The initial impact of AIDS on the lives of gay men was severe. Not only did gay men have to mourn the loss of loved ones but they also had to confront AIDS-phobia. The aftershock of AIDS is as scary but now there is more hope. In the early eighties, when AIDS first appeared, both the quality and the tabloid press spread inaccurate information about HIV and AIDS. 'Gay plague' was a term the tabloid press, in particular, bandied about. The after effect was that homophobia became more rampant. Attacks on gay men rose. AIDS-phobia, and by association fear of gay men, had the police infamously raiding gay venues wearing surgical gloves and masks. Information on HIV and AIDS has improved but the legacy of the original propaganda, that gay men started AIDS, remains. On hearing of the actor Brad Davies's death following complications because of his AIDS status a member of a men's group I was working in commented 'I didn't even know he was gay.'

Back then, for many, gay equalled AIDS. Today, the stigma stays. While it was political at the time to highlight that 'AIDS affects everyone'(the notoriously ineffective Health Education Authority's iceberg campaign comes to mind) the reality was that a disproportionate number of gay men were becoming infected with HIV. Now the breakdown of AIDS diagnoses shows that cases of AIDS are higher amongst gay men, which explains why a number of gay men-led organisations are calling for the re-gaying of AIDS, so that resources can be distributed proportionately to groups most affected.

At the beginning of the AIDS pandemic certain groups were identified as being high risk sections. This, in effect, was tantamount to looking for a scapegoat, which was found in disadvantaged and traditionally politically impotent sections of society: sex workers, intravenous drug users, gay men and Black people.

Here was this terrible disease with which, understandably, no-one wanted to be identified. The gay community attempted to diffuse some of the attention by identifying that HIV could and would affect everyone's life. The Black community, having to deal with the huge effects of racism on a day-to-day basis, having to convince society that we are as capable, as decent, as honest as everyone else, denied that HIV could impact on our lives and rejected the lie that AIDS originated in Africa. As a result, it did not truly take on board the gravity of the epidemic. It is understandable, albeit sad, that Black people would reject owning AIDS. After all, as Black people were accused of taking homes, jobs and benefits away from more deserving, and it was implied, white causes, we did not want to give the racists another excuse to hate us.

What is interesting is that the two portraits of Black people and of lesbians and gay men are almost polar opposites and it seems that the two never shall meet. The macho stereotype that is used to depict Black men could not be further away from the clichés that inaccurately make up representations of gay men. The sexually alluring and sexually intimidating cliché used to signify Black women could never tally with that of the notion of a sexless, swaggering lesbian. The effect is that Black people find themselves pressurised into adopting mannerisms, characteristics and actions that do not sit happily with them, but which continue to be the only outlets allowed them. Racism also shapes how others perceive Black people, feeding the already false views of race. Nevertheless, as with all stereotypes, there is some element of truth. While it may be true that a number of Black men are aggressive, strong and heterosexual, it is clearly not representative of Black men as a group. It never fails to amaze me that our society is able to base its reality on so little information.

Surely if these stereotypical perceptions were based on any reality then there would be no weak Black heterosexual men, 'feminine' lesbians or Black lesbians or Black gay men. And there are several very well known Black lesbians and Black gay men.

When Justin Fashanu, England's first one million-pound footballer player came out as a gay man the furore would have been less, it could be argued, had he been white. What Fashanu did was more than just applaudable and courageous. In the pages of the tabloid press he challenged simultaneously the notions of what popular assumptions perceived it meant to be a gay man and also allowed for a redefinition of what it meant to be a Black man. The perceptions that Black men traditionally meant a priapic *heterosexual* stud were being challenged proved hard to conceive. It was interesting that many white gay men championed Fashanu as a *gay* hero, without really acknowledging the difference of his race and welcomed him with open arms, something I took issue with as it ignored Fashanu's race.

I was a participant on a training course and found myself grouped with four white gay men. The course facilitator asked the group to name themselves by using something that united all members of the group. My group thought it easy to label itself the 'gay' group. I took issue with this. Being the only Black person on the course, I did not want the reality of my race overlooked or sidelined, as my self-perception as a Black gay man was shaped in a very different way to theirs as white gay men. I wanted them to realise that it was too easy for them to label me as gay and to pretend that there were no other differences between us. For me this was a way of asking me to decide if I was gay or Black first, something I was neither able nor prepared to do.

The Black community appeared more divided when Justin Fashanu came out. His commitment and affiliation to the Black community was questioned, in particular by Britain's best selling Black paper *The Voice*, as if being gay made him any less Black. In Black-only groups that I led following Fashanu's disclosure, it became evident that any anger they felt was not only based on their homophobia. For members of the group, not only had Fashanu come out to *The Sun* (a paper not known for its sympathetic approach when reporting on Black issues) but also it was felt that he was 'washing dirty linen in public'. Homosexuality has, inaccurately and unfairly, been viewed as evil by society. Homosexuality has falsely been labelled paedophilic, anti-family and anti-religion. The group members felt that Fashanu gave racists more reason to hate Black people, and was adding fuel to the fire for them. If there was one gay man amongst our ranks, then there would no doubt be more of them.

Visibility, or more accurately, invisibility was crucial at this time. Until this point there were very few if any positive representations of Black gay men. There have always been Black lesbians and gay men but our presence remained underground. It was known about though not widely talked about within the Black communities. Many words existed for lesbians and gay men that were created by the Black community, not words adopted from the west, which negates arguments that homosexuality is a western phenomenon.

When the group of Black people were pushed further about Fashanu it became clear that if the very masculine footballer Fashanu, hitherto (incorrectly perceived as) heterosexual, could be, and was, gay then it cast aspersions on their (hetero)sexuality. Their fear, like the heterosexual rugby players in *Sleeping with the Enemy*, was that others would think them gay.

It was put to them that they could use people doubting their heterosexuality to their advantage, to show society that there was much more to them than a restrictive view of Black heterosexuality, that Blackness could, and does, incorporate an infinitesimal quantity of equally valid possibilities. Unfortunately their heterosexism was so strong that to have anyone think that they were not heterosexual overrode all. They were unable to see how their tenacity was perpetuating myths about Black men, myths that the men in the group had so much difficulty confronting on a day to day basis.

In gay groups Black men felt good about Fashanu's decision to come out, and gained strength from it. Without a doubt the visibility of Black gay men has increased. Organisations such as Big Up, a sexual health organisation for Black men who have sex with men, work to raise the profile of Black gay men. This has not been without struggles. Funders appear keen to support projects for Black lesbians and gay men yet are keener to see the work justified by high numbers.

Black families and the Black community act as some barrier and protection against racism. They are both places where we know we can go to and call upon for support. The decision to come out in this safe space poses a difficult conundrum. Knowing that homosexuality is frowned upon at the best of times and condemned vehemently at the worst, it is understandable that

Black lesbians and gay men might be more reluctant to come out for fear of losing any protection from the racism surrounding us. White lesbians and gay men have some structures in place to provide them with support. It has only been recently that a small number of organisations have been set up to help Black lesbians and gay men empower themselves to tackle both racism and homophobia, without feeling that the two exist in isolation or conflict.

Black lesbians and gay men felt that mainstream groups and organisations did not meet their entire needs, and, from this dissatisfaction, Black Gay Men United Against AIDS and the Black Lesbian and Gay Centre were just two of the organisations established to redress the imbalances of suitable available services. Many generic gay agencies do not really address the reality of racism and Black organisations were rarely tackling the homophobia in its ranks. Those Black lesbians and gay men not fortunate enough to be in a town that has provisions for Black *and* gay groups may find themselves living seemingly two lives. They will go to different spaces for different reasons and feel they have to leave some aspect of themselves at the door.

In an ideal world, separate provisions for Black people and lesbian and gay men would be unnecessary. That ideal world is some time and distance away and, some might argue, would be a place where everyone was treated equally. Yet to try to make everyone equal would not only prove impossible without cloning or massacres but would be tantamount to denying both the huge differences amongst members of our society *and* the painful reality of discrimination. It negates the diverse experiences that exists amongst us, and fails to recognise that most of us have to cope with oppressions other than racism and homophobia. It is imperative that multiple oppression be addressed, based on anti-discriminatory practices, so that we all may feel 'complete'. It would mean working to address all other imbalances based on gender, marital status, ability, religious beliefs, age, etc. The active use of an equal opportunities policy, and I stress active, not merely a paper document, that is reviewed annually by external consultants is a start. I suggest external consultants as I believe organisations large or small can become precious and protective about themselves, thus being less able to tackle issues as clearly as required. The equal opportunity policy should also include clear procedures for tackling and sanctioning those who contravene the policy.

If this is not adopted what happens is that individuals feel disenfranchised and incomplete and they find themselves metaphorically floating from organisation to organisation trying to find a space where they feel comfortable. So, instead of getting the help they initially sought, valuable time is spent checking out, researching or testing organisations, so as to avoid having to face any painful oppressions.

A Black gay friend of mine who is living with AIDS tried several HIV organisations: first mainstream gay, then Black gay, then mainstream generic. He opted for the latter, as this was the place in which he felt most comfortable, where issues around oppression, and challenging them, were clear and thought out. He told me that he chose it because at his induction to the service one of the male volunteers challenged him about his sexist language. My friend explained that he was in other organisations where he was allowed much more unacceptable behaviour, as workers were afraid to challenge for fear of being accused of racism or homophobia. So while it is affirming and still necessary to have Black gay organisations it is not true that they are the panacea for all Black gay men, nor free of, or even aware of, issues of discrimination.

It is unfortunate still that many organisations do not see it as their duty to adopt anti-discriminatory practices in their services. This became clear to me when I was working as the outreach worker at the Black Lesbian and Gay Centre in London. Few days went by without our organisation receiving a call from an ostensibly white organisation wanting us to take on a client whom they felt ill equipped to offer a service. We also answered calls from Black organisations who had a lesbian or gay client who had issues they did not want to, or could not, tackle. What in effect was taking place was that the Black Lesbian and Gay Centre found itself in a position where it was trying to support those people that mainstream organisations had not made efforts to accommodate. It was easier, it seemed, for them to refer to another organisation than try to solve the issues themselves. While it is understandable that there may have been very genuine fears that the service offered might have been inappropriate, it rarely seemed as if all avenues were exhausted before the referral was made. Had anti-discriminatory practices been in place, where staff had been trained in, and were confident around issues of race and sexuality, these clients would have been able to approach whatever organisation they chose, anticipating quality service.

It would be good practice for all organisations to realise that all service users have a right to approach any agency of their choice and expect a service that is suitable to their needs and requirements,

If an organisation is established to provide a service to a specific section of society then it should be accountable for doing as it proposes. A drop-in service for Black women, for example, should be accessible for all Black women and not be placed on the third floor of a building that does not have adequate wheelchair access. With this in mind it would be essential to guarantee that equality of opportunity is promoted by ensuring that disadvantaged and/or underrepresented groups of women feel able to tap into the services.

I joined a men's group as a facilitator halfway through its twelve-week course. It became evident that the other facilitators had not even thought about adopting anti-discriminatory practices. The group had, in effect, become a white, heterosexual men's group. Black men and what the group believed were gay men, I learnt, had come to the group but, I assumed, feeling uncomfortable with the set up and culture, had obviously chosen not to return. When I asked the group members why they felt that these people did not revisit I was stunned by the replies from the members and even more so from the facilitators. Comments were diverse: the men who did not stay were not strong enough to take a joke; the group was open to any man; any man can come and join us; all men were treated equally and welcome to join.

It was not until the second round of the twelve-week sessions had started that more Black men and a few gay men began to attend the group.

However, this followed an exhausting and difficult two-month break. During these eight weeks the two other facilitators and I spent days formulating the new ethos of the group. We had to decide where we wanted to take the members and to establish if the project was successful only if we changed the views of the group's participants or merely got them to understand some of the views. Our main worry was how we were going to alter the very heterosexual and white set-up without alienating existing members, who on the basis of being men had every right to attend, and open the group to all men eligible to join.

Nevertheless it was clear to me that I would rather see the group fold before it became what it was previously, as I could go into many places where that atmosphere still prevails so I do not want to work in one. Nevertheless, I did not want the original members to feel that they, or their views, were being censored. The effect of this would be that they would not feel able to participate actively, which was crucial to the group's success. The group established, through open debate, a series of 'learning aids' to allow safe participation (the group of men, mostly raised in institutions, had had enough of rules). The voice of the minority was always heard. No major group decision was made on majority rule and had to be made unanimously.

In relation to other men who were eligible to join the group, we had to solicit actively men from Black groups and gay groups through intensive outreach sessions and leafleting. Training was arranged for us on diverse topics including addressing multiple oppression, discrimination, managing group dynamics and, finally, co-working and co-facilitation. The latter was difficult as it highlighted a lot of fears and concerns for the facilitators. It was painful, as complaints were made which had to be investigated before the men's group reconvened concerning what was felt to be collusion by certain facilitators with group members about another's suitability and ability to facilitate the group.

It was inevitable that there was going to be an outburst from the group that we were taking political correctness to an extreme, and given that I am both Black and gay much of this resentment was directed at me.

It is interesting that people often use political correctness when they feel something is being taken away from them. In fact, the opposite is quite true, in that something is being offered them; in this case the chance to meet and interact with people who come with different views and experiences which could improve their lives.

The response to the expected outburst from the group was the same as if the group had tried to create a hierarchy of oppression, if it felt we needed to address one thing before we could address another. It was somewhat fortunate that the topic we were tackling was around being stopped by police. I pointed out that police officers could not fail to see that I am male but that they would also see someone who is Black. I cannot separate the reality of this and this shapes how other people see me, and how I interact with others.

As a group of facilitators it was our role to ensure that everyone felt safe to be himself in the group and still manage to function with our diverse differences. So long as we are different we need to be recognised as being different. It would be foolish and optimistic to expect that a men's group, that had members who were Black, white, gay, heterosexual, survivors of abuse and many other disparate issues that made us what we are, would be without conflicting issues.

It would be equally foolish and optimistic to expect our society, with even greater diversity, to be without problems. What we can expect, and have a right to get, is that our problems are tackled taking our differences into account. In place of viewing differences as something frightening, as fear of the unknown makes the fear grow three-fold, difference ought to be celebrated, as this will demystify them and make them seem less scary. And maybe that Black man you crossed the road to avoid is more scared of you than you are of him.

Racism affects our perceptions of race issues. It shapes how we view our society. It is pervasive in the media. It is restrictive and limiting and wary of change, as this will affect the status quo and alter the power imbalances that allow racism to exist.

Yet there have been numerous examples that contradict the misconceptions about being Black but, as racism is so powerful, these misconceptions are still pushed at us. Invisibility, stereotypes and denial of the presence of racism all lead to racism, which in turn shape our views of sexuality. By this it is meant that stereotypes perpetuate myths that all Black people are heterosexual, to have this sense of reality debunked would cause problems. Firstly for those who are heterosexual to have to alter their sense of reality.

Secondly for those Black people who are lesbians or gay men to tackle their own learnt homophobia and heterosexism, to come to terms with a sexuality that they were told did not exist.

It could work in a similar vein with sexuality affecting race issues. Given that the perceptions of gay sexuality are almost invariably white, the belief that all lesbians and gay men are white could lead one's racism, internalised or not, to conclude that Black lesbians and gay men do not exist. Back again to invisibility, stereotypes and the denial of the existence of oppressions.

We cannot move forward until these issues are addressed and tackled. From that we need to work on those who are aware of their capacity to oppress, but instead of ensuring that this power is not abused, feel guilty for being in this position of privilege. As a result, those who are in a position to affect change remain as useful as those who deny that there is a problem around discrimination. Placating liberal guilt is often as wearing as tackling oppressive behaviour itself. Neither Black people nor lesbians and gay men should be doing either.

CHAPTER 5

In Her Best Interests? Working with Dangerous Women

Maggie Metcalfe

Introduction

Over the past 20 years research into women's crime has increased and developed. Prior to this, studies at best neglected analysis of women's crime and at worst reflected interpretations of the criminal behaviour of women based on stereotypical and discriminatory perceptions. These served to perpetuate the cultural values and constructs that control women in our society, and did little to address female crime or advise practitioners. These values and constructs are a long time in changing and still exist in statutory and community agencies that are involved with women and their behaviour.

Early feminist criminological studies have achieved some change in these perceptions but now appear limited in their conclusions. Women have no less a capacity than men for committing crime, but quantatively their criminal behaviour is less. However, women offenders, particularly serious offenders appear to resist and reject the criminal label and this is not helped by early feminist propositions that women are victims and that this in a sense 'excuses' their offending. It is clear that women are victimised and discriminated against in our culture. What also needs to be explored is how they can be enabled to understand and take responsibility for their offending but not for the additional stigmas associated with breaching the cultural boundaries that define them as 'proper women'. Until this happens the manifestations of women's 'distress' at their treatment by our culture will continue to be misinterpreted. Distress and protest demonstrated by women's offending is still pathologised with labels from the vocabulary of mental illness or social victimhood, and women often have little alternative but to 'sign up' to those definitions. Growth of such pathological beliefs can lead to increased stigmatisation and a continuation of anti-social/offending patterns. This can reduce the agencies involved in working with women offenders to 'firefighting' rather than exploring the origins of the behaviour. I hope in this chapter to outline not only the difficulties and issues that the probation service encounters in working with women offenders but also a way forward in developing effective practice in assessing dangerousness.

The Problem

It is a source of considerable frustration to probation officers working with women offenders to experience the inconsistencies in the way all agencies involved in the criminal justice system deal with women. There is, for example, a generally held myth that women offenders are treated more leniently than male offenders which requires examination.

In the study *Sentencing Women* (Home Office 1997) Hedderman and Gelsthorpe found that magistrates ascribed different motives to women, divided offenders into 'troubled' or 'troublesome', with most women falling into the former category, and found that appearance/demeanour influenced the court. There was consensus that women were expected to appear more 'respectful' than men. In addition, there was a reluctance to use financial penalties or deal with women defendants in a way that would have negative repercussions for their children, if they had any. This led to discharges or moving up the sentencing tariff to community disposals. The study found women were less likely to receive a custodial sentence however, and commented that it is difficult to find ways to challenge stereotypical pictures of women (and men), without ignoring the fact that they often have different needs and responsibilities.

Although courts and other criminal justice agencies may appear to take a more 'sympathetic' approach to women, they are in fact enforcing traditional gender stereotypes, denying the women's individuality and equality and making assumptions based on a notion of 'her best interests'. In effect, the court participates in a very powerful and controlling dynamic.

Equally, the criminal justice system can find it difficult at times to acknowledge that some women offenders present a risk and can be dangerous, to themselves and/or to others. In this way it does not allow women to take responsibility for their offending behaviour and give them a clear opportunity to work to change it and bring to the fore the many oppressive factors that are directly relevant to their offending. Courts will take into account mitigating factors concerning a woman's offending, i.e. abuse, domestic violence, economic pressure, isolation, family pressure etc., but in perceiving women as victims, lose sight of them as perpetrators.

The probation service is part of 'the system' and is not free of guilt in how it has operated with women offenders. Efforts have been made to develop gender conscious delivery to women clients. Put simply, the dilemma is often one of colluding with the criminal justice system's myths, stereotypes and prejudices or not gaining the best outcome for women clients. In reports we mitigate and we justify. We emphasise vulnerability and we disempower. We emphasise caring roles and reinforce stereotypes. We explore emotional factors and show the women as mad, not bad. It seems that whatever we do we risk reinforcing a damaging process. Even if we manage carefully not to collude, we can ignore the differences that surround male crime and female crime as I will go on to discuss, and the result of this can be that women get a distorted if not a damaging service.

Our delivery can be inconsistent or seriously flawed and initiatives have often been largely based on individual workers' commitment to women offenders rather than part of the fabric of the service and have thus not been integrated or evaluated.

Historical Perspective

The role of women needs to be seen in the context of their traditional position in society where men are active and in control of the 'public' sphere and women play a supporting, enabling role in the private domestic sphere. The responsibilities and tasks this requires from women is awesome. As a wife/partner and mother, women are responsible for raising the next generation with the proper moral values and if they fail the blame is theirs. Poor mothering or failure to comply with expectations is blamed for everything from delinquency to promiscuity. Male perpetrators of violent and sexual crimes against women frequently blame their female victims and are encouraged to do so. Likewise, young women are often notionally entrusted with the responsibility of keeping their male partners well behaved and off the streets.

This pressure confines women very firmly into sexual, social and domestic roles that are useful to their male counterparts (and uses men as domestic policemen!). This stereotyping disadvantages women who do not, or will not fit these roles. Since women have little power or influence to affect the public sphere which sets down the rules of society, the consequences for them of deviating from accepted norms has been extreme. As, for example, in the debate about lesbian mothers rights and fitness (Paris, 1993).

The Punishment and Control of Women

Women are punished formally by the courts. Informal punishment/control of women takes the form of domestic and sexual violence and the consequent fear of being the victim of violent crime in society (Hanmer, 1977).

The processes of punishment, both formal and informal, take place within the structure of a male dominated society designed to maintain traditional roles and traditional patterns of behaviour. Sanctions against women who deviate or offend are well entrenched and formidable.

The very processes and constraints designed to keep women controlled and in line with 'traditional' roles and behaviours are, often, fundamental factors relevant to their offending. Whether women are attempting to escape from the straitjacket of the stereotypes or manage and survive what is happening to them, the cost of accomplishing this change is great. Often the nature of their existence is that they are isolated from social networks and supports, and it is very difficult to manage the process of any change in themselves and their situation alone. Poverty, care, responsibilities and male control all contribute to isolation.

Women commit fewer crimes proportionately than men and there are no really gender-specific crimes (Smart, 1977). Recorded criminal behaviour is largely a male activity but one in which women do participate. Heidensohn (1987) has commented that studies confirm that what distinguishes the pattern of female from male criminality is its frequency, scope and seriousness, not essential qualitative differences.

Serious women offenders, however, often face a situation where they are seen as doubly deviant; abnormal for breaking the rules and 'unfeminine and unnatural' for breaking out of their conventional roles. As Carlen (1983) points out, not surprisingly women offenders are aware of this double punishment and increasingly see the criminal justice system as unjust and unfair in comparison to the treatment of their male counterparts. Aware of the differential treatment women receive, and with an understanding of the reasons why this happens, many probation officers find it difficult to predict what attitudes a court will take in relation to any individual women offender. Equally, as I will go on to illustrate, it can be just as difficult to chart the progress of the woman's own behaviour.

Issues for Practitioners Working with Women who Commit Serious Offences

If it is difficult, given the distortions in the criminal justice system, to establish a gender conscious approach to working with women offenders generally, it is even more problematic with women who commit serious violent or sexual offences. It could be argued that the main difference between male and female offenders is the power differential i.e. women have less power with which to exercise their potential, to meet their needs and purposes or to fulfil their aims and aspirations according to their abilities.

Our culture reflects power and control by one section of society, which exercises that power, at least in part, by establishing stereotypes underpinned by an assumption (made fact) of inferiority of the stereotypical groupings. Women are perhaps the largest grouping in this respect, with greater implications for black women and lesbian women since racism and homophobia come into play. Children are another large vulnerable grouping and it is often, when individuals are doubly powerless as female children, that the abuse of power begins for some women, and almost all women offenders.

This is not to say that, exclusively, females are damaged and abused in childhood, but the roles and expectations of males as they grow older vary from those of females, in terms of developing power, control and opportunity in their lives. The impact of abuse may be as powerful, but available strategies for dealing with it are not the same.

To excuse women's offending or the risk of harm they may present on these grounds is not a helpful or an effective way of approaching them. As Hilary Allen (1987) comments, the woman who commits a violent crime is a 'disturbing' person. She cuts across many of the expectations of the criminal justice system, and much of the idealism of feminism also!

Women cannot be treated differently to men in terms of acknowledging and taking responsibility for their offending, otherwise they are done a disservice and not given the opportunity to address their offending and the factors relating to it. It can also place them at risk. Such an approach reflects the social/domestic/legal controls they meet everyday, only this time it is the 'caring' social work profession that gives them the patronising message 'we know the system and we know what's best for you!'

Saradjian's (1998) research outlines that serious female offenders as children 'were cared for by, at best, incompetent, and at worst, actively malevolent parents', and many experienced major separations from parental figures. In addition, they had to at least partially meet the needs emotional, physical and sometimes sexual of their adult carers, thus being given very distorted but powerful messages regarding relationships between adults and children. Childhood abuse, combined with a lack of close significant supportive relationships with others inside or outside the family with which to compare their treatment, results in the child's isolation and the likelihood that they will begin to feel the abuse is their fault, they are bad and they are to blame. This is often reflected in the adult lives of women, particularly women offenders, since alternative/appropriate role models and support networks to challenge the distorted models they experience are lacking or unavailable to them. This can lead to 'enforced' attachment to their abusers, as the only one(s) who show 'interest' in them. Feelings of worthlessness and helplessness are reinforced and feelings of anger are suppressed, particularly in women since they learn, as they grow up, it is not as acceptable for women to express or act out such feelings as it is for their male counterparts. Eagly and Steffen (1986) report that women are more likely to feel guilt or anxiety regarding aggression and seek other behaviour options if available.

Saradjian found that the women she studied had difficulty in perceiving themselves as aggressive. These feelings had to be suppressed. This repression is important since Megargee (1966) describes how many extremely aggressive crimes are committed by those who repress their anger over a long period of time. The woman who sexually abuses children or commits other violent acts may have had many reasons to be angry and repressed them and Starr (1966) adds that severe repression of these feelings can lead to depression, schizophrenia, paranoia and psychopathy.

Many of the women offenders in Saradjian's study were sexualised through abuse at an early age, and this may have conveyed 'that the only source of esteem is through sexual contact' and this is reflected in their attitudes and behaviour as they mature through adolescence into adulthood and reinforced by female images open to them within our culture (i.e. women meet the sexual needs of men). The implications of such a powerful web of distorted perceptions is increased for young lesbian women trying to establish their sexual identity at such a time.

Positive adult social/sexual relationships can undermine and challenge previous experiences, but for many women who commit serious offences, this is not forthcoming and their adult lives are characterised by one or several abusive relationships.

Further life crises/stresses and violent experiences in adulthood can exacerbate the feelings of worthlessness, abandonment, low self esteem, etc., that can become part of many women offenders' existence. Over time, 'coping' strategies are developed to survive these experiences but these are necessarily distorted responses and rationalisations to try and manage what is in effect unmanageable. Maher and Curtis (1995) suggest that female violence usually arises after a lengthy period of violent victimisation by a male. Consequently, it would seem many violent female offenders tolerate abuse for considerable periods before expressing aggression. The fact that women traditionally have little opportunity to develop supportive social contacts outside the family means that they can often obtain little relief for their feelings and self image. They have also often learned that violence is an integral part of relationships and feel powerless in the face of this.

Many of the life experiences of women offenders, in particular those who experience extensive abuse from a very young age, are also predictive of psychological difficulties in adulthood (e.g. Finkelhor 1986; Wyatt and Powell 1988). Women's use of drugs and alcohol may dull these feelings of distress temporarily and may assist in disinhibiting some types of offending behaviour, though Saradjian found that the use of psychotropic substances rarely featured in the commission of the offences of the women sex abusers she studied. She concluded that the offence "becomes a means of 'self medication' to alleviate stress of distress" but that "when the woman is not able to abuse the child then the feelings of distress and tension are experienced and 'dealt with' in self harming ways". Consequently, from such conclusions we may have some indication as to the correlative, if not causative, factors that are involved in serious offending in some women which can inform risk assessments and offence focused work.

The issue of the victims targeted by violent women is an important one. Rungay (1999) suggests that because much female violence can be seen as primarily expressive of anger and frustration in relationships, the victim in such a scenario is more likely to be someone close to the perpetrator. Partners and children are most frequent victims of murder. Saradjian (1996) also found that female sex abusers were found to target their own children or those in their care. Rungay observed that women were less likely than men to target multiple victims. This tends to reflect the situational aspect of women's violence which is usually perpetrated when they are alone with their victim.

Attacks by females on acquaintances often occur where women have 'chosen' or are involved in a lifestyle that renders them vulnerable to strangers i.e. sex work, drug dealing etc. Violent responses then occur as a result of actual or perceived harm to the self. In both of the above situations, expectations of violence and abuse, involvement in a violent culture and an eventual loss of ability to tolerate further abuse are all important factors in the choice of victims. Rungay comments that "The conditions in which women engage in serious violence thus appear to be extreme" and all these issues are important when assessing risk to potential victims.

Risk Assessment

As a practitioner I have frequently found it difficult to 'predict' risk of serious offending by women. Previous offending is often scant and can be trivial if it exists at all. Wiksynski (1997) comments that violent males were more likely to have multiple previous convictions than women and also to have convictions for violence itself. If a more serious or prolific offending pattern exists, escalation of seriousness does not necessarily follow since women offenders, in my experience, can turn frustration or aggression upon themselves in a variety of ways – use of alcohol, drugs or violent self harm. Their pattern of behaviour, and who is at risk of it, becomes highly variable and apparently unpredictable.

Case Example

One woman, who I will call Joan, had an extremely damaged background as a child, as an adolescent and as an adult. Having become involved in several extremely abusive relationships with men, and having developed over time a chronic alcohol problem she had accumulated a prolific conviction list for relatively minor offences. She then began misusing both prescribed and illegal drugs which increasingly threatened her already precarious state of health as well as her emotional state. It seems that if ever a woman was a victim, she was, and although sometimes appearing the architect of her own misery, she was much more abused by others because of her vulnerability. She then began to commit violent offences which quickly escalated to the point where even the somewhat patronising attitude of the courts was tested and imprisonment was felt to be the only option. She therefore moved from victim to 'dangerous perpetrator' very swiftly and was dealt with accordingly.

It is very tempting at such a point to conclude that the woman cannot be helped and should be incarcerated for 'her own good'. I will own that, a feeling of betrayal and even fear was aroused in myself as worker and similar feelings were clearly engendered in court personnel. What we experienced then, was based on our own assumptions of how women should behave, and how we know men behave in similar life circumstances which is seen as the norm. This is the essential difficulty of understanding many serious women offenders who are at once both victim and victimiser and apparently unpredictable.

Assessing Risk

On the basis of practice experience, I would suggest that there are clear issues in applying 'standard' risk assessment proforma to women offenders; since such proforma are directed at male criminal behaviour and cannot be generally applied to female offenders. This is particularly critical in relation to women sex offenders, where Beckett (1994) and Saradjian (1995) have highlighted how the problems inherent in assessing male sex offenders are compounded with women by the lack of appropriate gender aware tools. They draw on research which amplifies the dangers of applying male models to women's behaviour.

Thorough investigation of the life experiences of women offenders can, however, provide significant indicators as to risk of harm or reoffending. In practice, I look for the following indicators:

1. Abusive experiences: particularly within significant relationships throughout life.
2. Absence of appropriate alternative role models/relationships or support networks throughout life.
3. Damaged and distorted perceptions of self and others, particularly in relationships, sex and sexuality.
4. Sense of powerlessness coupled with an inability to cope appropriately with lifestyle crises.
5. Isolation/entrapment as adult women as a result of being in abusive relationships, heavy childcare/family/domestic responsibilities.
6. Suppression or inappropriate expression of feelings, particularly anger, that can be triggered by life experiences and/or current situation.
7. Level of recognition (or absence) in women of the need for change and motivation to accomplish this.

8. Level of hopelessness in the face of difficulties and particularly in terms of confronting offending.
9. Level of denial of risky/offending behaviour.
10. Access to potential victims.

Women offenders are not usually part of the 'culture of crime', a major factor in women's criminal behaviour is personal experience past and present, exacerbated by a culture that entraps them and gives no opportunity to find a way out. Close examination as to how individual women are able to manage this, and the intense feelings it generates, allows us to identify at least to some degree the level of risk of serious offending or as importantly, the risk of self harm.

While I do not suggest that male offenders do not undergo similar experiences, the opportunities for men generally to take control within their adult lives (albeit conforming to masculine stereotypes where possible) and to gain support from peers is much greater. The fact that they do not always do this appropriately, and therefore may offend, informs risk assessments about male offenders, and is the point at which the culture of (serious male) crime parts company with culture per se.

Women in Denial

Issues relating to perpetration of offences include denial, distortion, lack of empathy and use of disinhibitors. Denial of offending in all its forms is understandable, explainable but not excusable, and is a more significant issue for serious women offenders than for their male counterparts. Women have to feel enabled to disclose feelings associated with denial which means they have to confront feelings of shame, loss of respect, guilt, self blame and wider consequences from society. This closely parallels the issues faced by male offenders. However, it is generally more acceptable for men to be physically and sexually aggressive than women and women offenders face, in addition, the prospect of the loss of their 'female identity' so 'valued' by our culture. This will be all the more oppressive for lesbian and black women confronted with homophobia and racism since they have so much more to lose. They can be labelled 'doubly inferior' (black) or 'abnormal' (lesbian) and therefore vulnerable to additional oppression by a culture dominated by prejudiced values. Denial of serious offending for both men and women is complex, and requires distorted thinking, lack of empathy and a massive fear, suppressed or otherwise, of the consequences of disclosure in terms of survival. Denial in serious women offenders can be all the more solid because they will feel by giving up denial they are making themselves vulnerable to further intense victimisation and oppression not only for their offence(s) but for their 'unfeminine' behaviour. They perceive the need to cling to their denial as essential, in order to survive. The presence of such complex and strong denial is a significant obstacle to work on offending and may be a crucial indicator of risk.

Women who commit serious offending may not be quite as self focused as male offenders but the temporary 'relief' gained by committing the offence, or self harming, can develop into a tantalising cycle of behaviour which, given perceived, if not actual, lack of alternative options reflects not only a degree of risk but a focus for urgent intervention. There is no 'checklist' for assessing the risk of serious women offenders or predicting their frequency of type of offending. The points I have outlined are only a base for judgement. Saradjian (1996) provides a more detailed analysis in relation to female sex abusers, but points out assessment is an art, not a science, and there is no 'unique formula'. A judgement has to be made by the assessor and this should be made in the light of the maximum information available on the issues that are significant to serious *women* offenders. It is crucial that it also reflects clear knowledge and awareness of the oppressive experiences of women, their differential treatment within our culture, and the impact of this on women.

Engaging with Serious Women Offenders

In engaging with women offenders on risk assessments and offence focused work, there are a number of important factors to be considered. One study of probation practice illustrated how office environment, poverty, family demands/responsibilities and the largely masculine based model of the supervisory process and its requirements all militate against women offenders being able to engage in a process of work on their offending and their situation. It concluded:

> *The importance of practicalities can hardly be overestimated. Best practice means organising a reporting schedule that facilitates cooperation, taking account of domestic responsibilities in the same way as employment.*
>
> (Kemsall and Wright, 1994)

Issues such as these are crucial if women, particularly serious women offenders, are to work on their offending more effectively. It is not a question of 'preferential' treatment, it is a simple matter of paying attention to the situation of women and responding in a way which makes it easier for them to engage. Obstacles to this practice may be influenced by prejudice and oppression.

It we are successful in getting women offenders to report, the next task is to engage with them. It has been suggested that for many women, relationships means subordination. (Kemsall and Wright, 1994). Thus confrontative techniques are likely, especially with women offenders, to further entrench all those aspects of attitude/behaviour that need to change in order to reduce risk. An empathic relationship, with clear boundaries, is necessary to elicit the necessary information and enable change. This does not preclude challenge since, 'challenging the woman's beliefs and reasoning, and thereby offering alternatives to her set pattern of attitudes and beliefs, is likely to aid therapy' (Saradjian, 1994).

Women sex offenders perhaps present some of the most critical dilemmas since most of the research, models and intervention that inform our practice are based largely on male sex offenders. While the issues may be similar for both genders, the factors that relate to them are often different and the interventions should reflect that difference as I have observed. Additionally, the impact on the worker may be more distressing since hearing these perpetrators stories challenges some of our most fundamental assumptions about women's roles. For women workers it is no longer possible to use gender stereotypes to distance the worker from the possibilities of behaviour. The impact of all this can be excessive antipathy towards the offender.

Almost all women sex offenders feel they are powerless, no matter how powerful they may be perceived to be by others. In this way there are parallels with many male sex offenders but, given the traditional power imbalance between gender in society, the powerlessness experienced by both male and female sex offenders are contextually very different. Given the relative difference in socialisation, the way men and women are perceived in society and the different roles and stereotypes on offer to each gender, men are inevitably in a position to make other choices – they have more power to do so and in any case their 'bad behaviour' is more 'natural' to males. Also, men are expected to take the sexual initiative and define what is appropriate activity.

Women have fewer options and are normally more constrained in the choices they feel they can make. Therefore it is likely that serious offending by women offenders represents a more fundamental and desperate act and, as a consequence, can seem more frightening and alarming to the woman herself. This reinforces denial, but can be undermined if women offenders feel empowered in a relationship where they feel confident and safe in disclosing 'shocking' information. This is not reflected in their general treatment by the criminal justice system and often other agencies who see such offenders as having 'crossed a line' and in general a harsh, often punitive reaction reflects the woman's own fear, alarm and uncertainty.

Moving on in Practice

As practitioners, this is the dilemma we can face in working with women who commit serious offences: punishing them because we do not want to confront the discomfort their crime generates for us, or 'explaining' the crime by working often only on their victim status as opposed to their victimiser status. Either way, offending behaviour can fail to be addressed and any informed risk assessment is not possible. Child protection and public protection issues will not therefore be safeguarded and women offenders will not be given the opportunity to address their offending and factors related to it and hopefully move on.

To begin the process of challenge, we have to separate the strands of the actual criminal offence and the perceived 'crime' of not conforming to the ideals of womanhood. Practitioners have to address the denial in themselves if they are to work with serious women offenders on the same issue. These issues have to be understood, academically and emotionally by those working with such women offenders.

An equally difficult aspect of working with serious women offenders is the split present in being a victim as well as a victimiser. Eldridge (1994) talks of walking the tightrope of the victim/perpetrator divide and this expresses the dilemma precisely. Saradjian (1996) likewise advises that issues of victimhood must be dealt with to enable discussion of offending behaviour. What is equally important is that a focus is held on the woman's own responsibility for her actions. To do less is to act out of prejudice and stereotyping.

On the basis of my experience I would offer the following suggestions to colleagues:

1. Working with women offenders exclusively as victims can increase the sense of powerlessness or entrapment and possibly reinforce patterns of distorted thinking and offending behaviour. It can increase risk, by omitting to give women the opportunity to take responsibility for their violent behaviour.
2. Women offenders need to explore and understand their own victimisation and how this has affected attitudes and beliefs to enable them to justify their own perpetrator behaviour and take responsibility for this.
3. A woman's relationship with the worker is important in achieving change. She has to feel safe, be aware of clear boundaries to a relationship that offers an appropriate alternative model to many previous relationships and one that empowers by giving space for the acknowledgement of emotions and for 'making sense' of what she has done and what has been done to her. The gender of the worker is important in this respect. Given the relational and situational aspects of women's violence and the fact that much of their abusive experiences will have been perpetrated by males, women workers can have a key role to play in providing safety in a relationship with which to explore issues of victimisation, denial, destructive feelings and assist in developing

alternative options in terms of female identities/models and behaviour and how these can be achieved.

This does not exclude men from working with women offenders, but until some women offenders have abandoned the distorted coping/survival strategies based on attempts to defuse or moderate the violence/abuse they have learnt to expect from men, then this dynamic is likely to be re-enacted in the working relationship. From my experience the timing of any engagement with male workers is important and can be positive if women offenders are empowered to use this situation to experience alternative male behaviour which is not oppressive and which they can manage appropriately. Much will depend on the knowledge, awareness and ability of the male worker involved.

4. Since much female violence erupts under extreme conditions and often after a lengthy period spent attempting to cope or survive difficulties, confrontative challenge can exacerbate this situation and even increase risk. Women nevertheless need to be challenged regarding their offending and this can often be accomplished through exploration of consequences of violent behaviour to all concerned, and developing awareness of their power to choose other options, however limited. Given that women tend to commit violent offences in more private surroundings, whether we like it or not, they will make the decision to offend alone, and work on their denial, their decision making and their self protection is more likely to assist them in such situations.

5. Safety is also important if women are to take advantage of support networks that are crucial if they are to achieve changes in their situation and lifestyle, and so such supports, at least initially, need to be from other women, women's community organisations etc.

6. The process of working with serious women offenders may need a level of counselling that probation officers cannot deliver. Referral to clinical psychologists may be appropriate and preparation for this may be a task for the supervising officer as well as ensuring that perpetrator behaviour is addressed as well as victimisation. Anger management techniques that are frequently advocated for male violence may not be suitable for women. Women do appear to manage their anger over lengthy periods, but almost inevitably this will fail as a problem solving strategy because they remain in the situation that gives rise to destructive feelings. Men generally have more power and opportunity to influence or control their situation, women much less so. Standard anger management work with men works towards acceptance of responsibility for violence and techniques to exercise self control through a variety of strategies. Hamberger and Potente (1994) suggest that chronically abused women who exhaust their ability to control or suppress their anger are assisted

more in learning skills in positive self-assertion and self-protection than strategies in self-control.

7. Relapse prevention should enable an offender to identify risk in themselves or situations and lapses that can lead to re-offending. This work can empower women to recognise and take appropriate actions in the situations that raise their vulnerability, but this is only possible once they have the skills, motivation and support networks to accomplish this. Women offenders, unlike their male counterparts, need to understand how they can manage the discrimination and abusive attitudes directed towards them that are endemic to our society. Women will have to develop relapse prevention strategies to deal with this if they are not to remain vulnerable to collusion with a system which can seek to re-victimise them.

Conclusion

Working with serious women offenders is a somewhat daunting task since re-victimisation and oppression can be and is perpetrated by agencies working with women and women offenders within the community, including criminal justice agencies. As workers, we are responsible for our own practice and behaviour in working with such women offenders. This practice needs to be based on a clear knowledge and understanding of the disadvantaged position of women in our culture and a determination to develop gender conscious practice integrating both feminine and masculine concerns. It has been suggested that where agency resources are restricted, probation officers operate on a masculine understanding of female offending and criminality, and utilise traditional perceptions of womanhood to deal with women offenders (Kemsall and Wright, 1994). This is not only poor practice, it is very risky practice not least in terms of protection of the public. We need to hold onto the principle of gender conscious practice, and employ strategies and interventions that take account not only of women's victim status and problem configurations, but also their aggression and violence and the historical and situational context of these behaviours. Such an approach could also inform practice with male offenders by exploring the differences in criminal behaviours between the genders in a more informed way rather than by judging seriousness and risk on the basis of stereotypes.

References

Allen, H. (1987) *Gender Crime and Justice*. Carlen, P. and Worrall, A. (Eds). Milton Keynes/Philadelphia: Open University Press.

Beckett, R. (1994) Assessment of Sex Offenders, in Morrison, T., Erooga, M. and Beckett, R. (Eds) *Sexual Offending Against Children*. London: Routledge.

Carlen, P. (1983) *Women's Imprisonment*. London: Routledge and Keegan Paul.

Eagle, A.H. and Steffen, V.J. (1986) Gender and Aggressive Behaviour; a Meta-analytic review of the Social Psychological Literature. *Psychological Bulletin*.

Eldridge, H. (1994) Personal Communication in Saradjian J. (1998) *Women who Sexually Abuse Children*. Chichester: John Wiley and Sons.

Finkelhor, D. (1986) *A Source Book on Child Sex Abuse*. Beverley Hills, CA: Sage.

Hamberger, L.K. and Potente, T. (1994) Counselling Heterosexual Women Arrested for Domestic Violence: Implications for Theory and Practice, *Violence and Victims*.

Hanmer, J. (1977) *Violence and the Social Control of Women*. Mimeo: British Sociological Association.

Heidensohn, F. (1985) *Women and Crime*. London: Macmillan, New York University Press.

Heidenshon, F. (1987) *Gender, Crime and Justice*, in Carlen, P. and Worrall, A. (Eds). Milton Keynes/Philadelphia: Open University Press.

Home Office Research Study 170 (1997) *Sentencing Women*. Hedderman, C. and Gelsthorpe, L. (Eds).

Kempsall, H. and Wright, L. (1994) Feminist Probation Practice: Making Supervision Meaningful. *Probation Journal*. V:41: No. 2.

Maher, L. and Curtis, R. (1995) In Search of the Female Urban 'Gangsta': Change, Cultural and Crack Cocaine, in Price, B.R. and Solokoff, N.J. (Eds) *The Criminal Justice System and Women; Offenders, Victims and Workers*. New York: McGraw-Hill.

Megargee, E.I. (1966) Uncontrolled and Overcontrolled Personality Types in Extreme Anti-social Aggression. *Psychological Monographs; General and Applied*, No. 611.

Paris, P. (1993) Pretended Families in Mcgauhey, C. and Buckley, K. (Eds) *Sexuality, Youth Work and Probation Practice*. Sheffield: Pavic.

Rumgay, J. (1999) Violent Women: Building Knowledge-based Intervention Strategies in *Good Practice in Working with Violence*. Kempshall, H. and Pritchard, J. (Eds). London: Jessica Kingsley.

Saradjian, J. (1998) *Women who Sexually Abuse Children*. Chichester: John Wiley and Sons.

Smart, C. (1977) *Women, Crime and Criminology*. London: Routledge and Keegan Paul.

Starr, A. (1966) *Human Aggression*. Harmondsworth: Penguin Books.

Wilson, E. (1983) *What is to be done about Violence Against Women?* Harmondsworth: Penguin Books.

Wiczynaki, A. (1997) *Child Homicide*. London: Medical Media.

Wyatt, G.E. and Powell, G.J. (1988) *Lasting Effects of Child Sexual Abuse*. Beverley Hills CA: Sage.

CHAPTER 6

Straight Talking on Sexuality

Ted Perry

Introduction

This chapter has been written by a well experienced, heterosexual male main grade probation officer. It is largely based on experience and expresses much of what I do *not* understand, rather than what I do. Hopefully, it reflects the struggle that I have experienced, and still do experience, in trying to understand and work with people of a differing sexuality to my own. This struggle is one that each male heterosexual practitioner experiences, but rarely acknowledges and speaks about. We pay lip service by making ritualised anti-discriminatory statements believing that this enables us to work in a sexually neutral manner. In reality, we tend to continue to do our thinking on the assumption of heterosexual normality but our life experiences trap us into conventional thinking and practice when we are working with people whose very sexuality defies convention.

I am not an academic and I have no knowledge of hard research or written material that throws light on how we can break out of the trap of convention. I am not developing the thoughts of others or suggesting new forms of theory and practice that will provide answers for practitioners who work with gay offenders. There are no new quick fix techniques that will help to break down the barriers between worker and offenders.

My writing is essentially about my own experience of working with gay sex offenders which I believe has helped to further my understanding of the routine victimisation of all gay males in a community where heterosexuality is seen as normality. My understanding is still far from complete and I am unable to put my hand on my heart and say that I can now work with gay men in a non-oppressive way. All I can say is that I believe that I am still taking part in a struggle to which all heterosexual practitioners must apply themselves if they are to help gay abusers to change their behaviour towards others.

Before I start, I should perhaps warn the reader that much of this chapter may seem to be contrary to conventional wisdom and it may be easy for me to be misunderstood. So, to make myself absolutely clear I will begin by restating three principles of good practice in working with sex offenders that normally apply regardless of the sexuality of the offender:

- Sexual abuse is an act of violence.
- It is committed against the will of the victim.
- It causes damage to the victim.

These are basic principles that we learn as novices in working with sex offenders and over time we absorb them so thoroughly that we tend never to consciously think about them. I remember that they made good sense to me when, many years ago, I chose to work in what was, for me, a new discipline, and they have served me well ever since. But, from time to time, a case crops up which tests out these assumptions. When this occurs, it is usually one where the conventional rules just don't quite seem to apply and I find myself almost in an impasse in trying to move an offender on in accepting responsibility.

Case Material

The first time I can recall this happening to me was about five years ago when I first met Brian in prison. It was a through-care case that I had inherited, and I had met him several months into a seven-year sentence for his umpteenth conviction for the sexual abuse of boys. He was an isolated man who trusted nobody in the system and was evasive and resistant in talking about his offending. Working with him was not going to be easy.

Brian was languishing in the Vulnerable Prisoners Wing at a category 'B' prison and had been written off by everybody. Attempts had been made to assess him but he refused to take the process seriously and, to make matters worse, he was actually saying that his victims consented to sex with him and, as they enjoyed the experience, they had not been significantly harmed. This was unacceptable to the professionals in both the prison and probation services who all wrote him off and were prepared to abandon him until the incentive of parole would cause him to change his tune. Unfortunately, Brian was so used to institutional life that he was more comfortable inside prison than out. He didn't care about parole and it suited him perfectly to be left alone and for his offending to be ignored. It also left him in the classic position of being allowed to continue to distance himself from his behaviour, fantasise and reinforce his abusive sexual beliefs and attitudes without any more questions being asked.

This left me with a problem. I didn't have the luxury of being able to ignore him. Whenever he was released from prison, I would be the one who would have to supervise him and, if his distorted beliefs and attitudes remained intact, it would be too late for me to make up lost ground in the community. I would then be responsible for managing a high-risk offender in the community and, if I wanted to protect anyone, I certainly would not have been able to do it by persuading him that he presented a danger to boys and that it would be in his interests to change. If I were to be able to achieve anything with him, I would have to start whilst he was still in prison and begin by trying to understand the distorted logic of his thinking as a means of getting some common ground on which we could work.

There was clearly no point in arguing with him so, after a couple of visits that got nowhere, I started him talking about himself. I was trying to get him to associate his own experiences of being sexually abused as a boy with those of his own victims in the hope that this would enable him to identify the feelings of the victim through his own knowledge of the damage that had been caused. However, Brian wouldn't budge. He still insisted that he had co-operated with his abuser and enjoyed the sexual relationship and it hadn't done him any damage, had it? But, if he hadn't been damaged by these experiences, how come he was serving a seven-year sentence?

I kept him talking and soon realised that he genuinely was relating his own experiences to those of his victims but he was coming to it from a different direction from myself. Brian was a gay man and, as a boy when his sexuality was developing, his first formative sexual experiences were with boys at a childrens' home. As a deprived child, these experiences were just about the only source of comfort and pleasure to him and were the nearest thing he ever got to an expression of love. From infancy, Brian's abusive sexual experiences were normalised and now he could not allow himself to see his own sexual experiences as damaging and, if he believed they were not, how could I argue with him? To him they were acts of normal gay sexual behaviour and any suggestion from me at that stage that there are issues of power differential that may have made the relationship both illegal and inappropriate, would have caused him to dismiss me as yet another homophobic oppressor. Although I couldn't share his reasoning, I had to leave it unchallenged as I only had what made sense to Brian to go on and, whatever I believed, I had to accept *his* reality.

At the age he was at the time, he would have had little awareness of sexuality and I would imagine that he would have got very little help with it from the staff at the childrens' home who were largely a part of the abusive environment themselves. Every learning experience he would have had would have been a contradiction between the socially structured messages that homosexuality is wrong and the feeling that gay sex feels good and comforting. He would also learn that sex has only a physical expression and has nothing to do with a caring relationship. Brian would not have seen his experiences as exploitative or damaging or that they came at an inappropriate age and that they began to shape his attitudes towards adult/child sex at a very early stage. This problem was compounded by the fact that at times when he was able to return home, his father would also sexually abuse him. As he was by this time sexually experienced, he did not see this as abusive either and he was quite content to be his father's sexual partner. At this early age, he had also learned two confusing lessons. Firstly, the acceptable one that there is nothing wrong with gay sexual relationships and, secondly, the unacceptable one that there is nothing wrong with adult/ child sexual relationships.

This was, and still is, normality to Brian. As a child he had been given no opportunity to learn the validity of his sexuality. He had also been given no opportunity to discover it in a safe, caring environment and this had allowed others to exploit him for their own sexual gratification. This had done him tremendous damage and has now left him locked in a vicious circle of being unable to restructure his thinking, beliefs and attitudes. At a thinking level, and when it suits him, he is capable of acknowledging that what he does to boys is wrong. But when it comes to controlling his behaviour, he is stuck with the distorted attitudes that his childhood experiences have etched on to his brain and he can no more give them up than I can give up breathing.

When I first met Brian, I was as confused about him as he was about himself. Like most of my heterosexual colleagues, I stuck to the basic principles that underpin my work with sex offenders which, presumably, had originally been scribed by heterosexuals in the context of heterosexual normality. As I slowly developed more understanding of sexuality, I gradually began to see that the application of the conventional rules to challenging Brian's beliefs and attitudes did not work.

I am now getting into deep water and, again, before anyone begins to misunderstand what I am saying, I had better make two important but obvious points. Firstly, Brian does not abuse boys because he is gay. He does so because it meets his emotional and sexual needs which is something that he cannot achieve through peer relationships and also because he has the power to do so. Secondly, it is not all right for him to abuse because he is gay or because he himself was sexually abused at a time when his emotional needs at the time were not being appropriately met. His beliefs and attitudes are his own and he speaks for himself and not for all gay child abusers. But, whenever I work with one, I have to shift my thinking and try to understand why his beliefs and attitudes have been shaped in this way.

So how do I get myself in a position where I, as a male heterosexual worker, can operate with a gay male sex offender in an anti-oppressive manner that effectively protects children? I wish that I had a simple answer, but like all heterosexual males (and possibly females), I struggle in working with gay offenders. For most of my life I have been so indoctrinated by a heterosexual concept of normality that I am now locked into a straight-jacket of conventional thinking. I still find myself reverting to the same old conventional assumptions, knowing full well that working with gay men requires more than an element of culturally lateral thinking.

When we struggle with what we don't understand, it is easy to take the line of least resistance and play it safe. In working with sex offenders, it is easy to state the conventionally obvious and then conveniently brush the issues of sexuality aside. But we have to keep the offender's sexuality and sexual development in mind if we are to understand his offending and try to deal with it effectively. It is also important to consider sexuality when working on the issues of victimisation of the boys who have been abused. This can be vital in working with the offender on victim awareness and the development of victim empathy.

This issue arose in the case of Kevin where the experiences of both victim and perpetrator were important in understanding his offending. At the time of the offence, both victim and perpetrator were struggling to understand their own sexuality and learn how to be able to live and express themselves as gay males in a hostile environment. Their respective struggles eventually drew them together into a relationship that developed into a confused and contradictory melange of caring and abuse.

Kevin was a mature, adult man who appeared to be living happily with his wife and two children. He was working in a responsible job that was hard, lonely and demanding but it enabled him to earn a good living and support his family well. But whilst he was outwardly behaving in a conventional and socially acceptable way, he was really a gay man struggling in trying to live in a caricature of a 'respectable' heterosexual family relationship.

As time passed, Kevin gradually started to suspect his true sexuality and, eventually, to acknowledge it to himself. His female partner, his children and his home still remained important to him and he was prepared to go on living clandestinely in his conventional role without even his partner suspecting that there was a problem. Predictably, he wasn't comfortable in living with the lie that his entire life became and his only relief was to find an occasional physical outlet where he could express his gay sexuality in casual relationships with male strangers. Of course, he didn't feel safe in doing this and each encounter with a stranger presented a risk to him. He didn't know who he was with, how the unknown partner was likely to behave and, for him, sex degenerated into an episodic, swift encounter with a stranger picked up in a public toilet or met in the local cruising grounds. No names and no intimacies were exchanged and there was certainly no emotional content in the association. It was pure sexual gratification between two consenting gay males – all very clinical and all very secretive. But there was also a new dimension to these sexual relationships for Kevin. His lifelong experience of sex had been based on heterosexual relationships where the balance of power would almost invariably lie with the man. But, in sex with a man, he found that this was rarely the case for himself.

Although he was usually as physically strong as his casual gay partners, they were almost always more experienced and confident and, in every case, were a completely unknown quantity to him. It takes little imagination to see how unsure of himself he would feel and how threatening each experience would be for him.

Whilst Kevin was trying to deal with the problems of understanding his own sexuality, he was not to know of a young boy who was living nearby and sharing his struggle. Adrian was 14 years old and had begun to see himself as different from the other boys he knew at his school and in the neighbourhood. He had difficulty in understanding what was wrong but, somehow, he just didn't seem to fit in, particularly when he began to become more aware of his sexual development. He found himself withdrawing from contact with the other boys, somehow sensing that they were not to be trusted and he certainly did not feel comfortable in what was seen as the normality of boy/girl relationships.

Adrian was isolated and, as often happens with isolates, he became vulnerable. Other boys rejected him and he became a loner and a victim of minor bullying. He also gradually realised that, when other boys were starting to show an active interest in sex, his own sexual interests were different. The other boys were interested in the physically well-developed girls at school or the silicon breasted 'Baywatch' actresses on television. He preferred his own fantasies about the younger male teachers at school.

He had only a vague notion of homosexuality. It may have been touched on in the sex education of the National Curriculum but it had not been addressed with any real commitment. (After all, we can't have teachers promoting homosexuality, can we?) So how was Adrian to learn what he needed to know? From his peers at school? His parents? His teachers? He had already picked up messages from these people about homosexuality before and they had been far less than helpful. He had only heard expressions of revulsion, ridicule and condemnation and had rarely seen a single positive image of a gay man in the media. From his experience, the whole world saw gay sexuality in terms of abnormality. There was no reassurance for him and it was not safe for him to be different.

So there was nowhere for Adrian to go and he was left to struggle with sorting out his sexuality for himself. But, as most of us know, when we try to do anything on a DIY basis without proper guidance, we inevitably begin by making the most basic mistakes. Adrian was no exception. He started by reading whatever he could find on gay issues in the popular press and, in particular, in his mother's women's magazines. The messages that he got from these sources were inconsistent and sometimes of doubtful accuracy and, at times, were sufficiently homophobic to confuse and endanger him even further. One particular article told him about how gay men would sometimes meet each other in public toilets and it occurred to him that this may present him with an opportunity to experiment with sex with gay men who he assumed he could trust. He believed that if he found a sexual partner in this way, he could learn about sex safely and that it would also help to resolve his confusion.

The magazines that he had been reading had not addressed the more basic issues such as the value of relationships, peer relationships, safe sex and they had not prepared him for the dangers of sexual exploitation. So, armed with nothing more than the fantasies about school teachers and the wisdom of the popular press, Adrian set off for his first sexual experience in a town centre public toilet where, almost inevitably, he met Kevin.

Now he could have done much worse than to meet Kevin who does possess some caring qualities and is a reasonably sensitive man. Unfortunately, Adrian was exactly what he was instinctively looking for; an easy, vulnerable male who was looking for a casual, no commitment sexual relationship and one where Kevin could enjoy the familiar advantages of being in a position of power and control.

Kevin was the first man to have the opportunity to abuse Adrian. He took him to the local woods where there was a quick, furtive act of masturbation following which Kevin gave him a couple of pounds. Although they were to meet occasionally in the future when Kevin would abuse him again, the real damage was done on this first occasion through Adrian being encouraged by the 'success' of his experience. He became a regular visitor to the toilets and eventually became well known to virtually every abuser of boys for miles around.

Adrian had been a willing partner and had enjoyed the experience just as Brian had all those years before. It is true that he had been harmed but not in the conventional sense of being damaged by the trauma of non-consensual sexual abuse. The damage was done by a number of perpetrators who had subjected him to what, in his perception, were experiences that liberated him from the constraints of a conventional but alien sexuality. He felt accepted and rewarded by these relationships but was oblivious to the fact that most of the perpetrators were exploiting him for the gratification of having sex with under-age boys. Adrian was both abused and corrupted and, in all probability, is now as confused about himself and his sexuality as he has ever been and he will still not know where to go for appropriate support and help. All that will happen now is that Kevin will go on to a prison sex offender group and, hopefully, learn how his behaviour has contributed to the damage done to this unfortunate boy. But this does not address issues of sexuality or meet the needs of gay men and boys. It is also of little use to Adrian whose needs lie in addressing his issues of sexuality in a safe, supportive environment. This is important in the case of all male victims and survivors regardless of their sexuality. Working with the perpetrator in itself rarely helps the victim directly and, in fact, in cases of boys such as Adrian, it is a matter of closing the stable door after the horse had bolted. He needed the help long before he even thought of taking his disastrous leap in the dark.

Application

I must once again emphasise that these are the views of a well-conditioned heterosexual and, perhaps I may not have got it all entirely right. But, if I am struggling to make sense of sexuality, then so do all heterosexual male workers. We can all acknowledge at a head level the importance of anti-homophobic practice and we can all try to impress and to try to make ourselves feel good by trotting out all the anti-discriminatory clichés. We can learn them by rote and regurgitate them on cue as a means of trying to impress our gay and lesbian colleagues. Better still, we can also use them to score points over our less informed or less vociferous colleagues in this competitive sport of working with sex offenders.

The simple fact is that none of us really understands what we are not and, if we are honest, we will all acknowledge our personal struggle. The case examples I have given from my own practice must reflect my own confusion but I hope that they also illustrate that better practice can develop from us working honestly and within our limitations and by continually attempting to extend our understanding of what is beyond our personal experience.

It is not simply a matter of giving a better performance when working with male abusers of boys. It goes beyond this into a greater understanding of the problem of all gay males who are all victims themselves at some stage in their development. Many are victims of direct sexual abuse and exploitation but many more must surely be victims of a system that, as in the case of Adrian, gives lip service to equality. In practice, it gave him nowhere to go at a time when he was struggling with his own identity both as a male and as a sexual being. Until the thinking of all heterosexual males such as myself can develop, then there can be little hope for the protection of vulnerable boys other than by the repression and control of male abusers who are likely to be gay themselves.

So where do we go from here? It seems to me that we heterosexuals have very little understanding of sexuality. We never have to think about it! Although I have spent much of the past few years trying to understand sexuality, it has only just occurred to me that I know more about gay sexuality than my own. Gays and lesbians have had to consider issues of their sexuality out of necessity if they are to survive in a homophobic society. But we heterosexuals have had the luxury of being able to take our sexuality for granted. This has left us in ignorance of our own sexual behaviour of diversity and with little understanding of those who differ from us.

We still have much to learn from the experiences of gay and lesbian people. We need to learn how to think in terms of there being no normality and that knowledge and acceptance of diversity enriches us all and promotes understanding of the behaviour of ourselves and others. When we learn to understand how our differing sexuality develops in the context of our own experiences then we may be able to relate better to other people regardless of sexual preference.

We also have to acknowledge that the majority of offences of sexual violence have probably been committed by heterosexual males and that we are still not addressing properly the issues that lie at the cusp of heterosexuality, gender and violence. We need to know more about this, as, yet again, we cannot work effectively with what we do not understand. But it is difficult to know where to start in furthering our knowledge of sexuality as it impacts on working with sex offenders. In thinking through this chapter, I have become conscious of the lack of written material on this subject and have had to rely heavily on experiential learning. Because of this I am making many assumptions that are not backed up by the research that needs to be done. However, this does not mean that there is no literature worth reading. In understanding the problems of Adrian, I have been helped by Terry Sanderson's book, *Stranger in the Family*, which is a guide to heterosexual families in dealing with their confusion when a boy identifies himself a gay. In working with gay offenders, *Pink Therapy*, edited by Davies and Neal, has helped to give me confidence and has affirmed much of my experiential learning.

Working with issues of sexuality is not easy when dealing with sex offenders and it becomes more difficult for heterosexuals who have not had to face up to the challenge to our perspective. This is a very threatening arena and most of us choose to ignore it. If we continue to do so then we lack knowledge and are dis-empowered. But, as we gain in knowledge we grow in confidence, our professional boundaries are extended and we become more able workers.

CHAPTER 7

Violence, Sexuality and Gay Male Domestic Violence

Graeme Vaughan

Over the past number of years, there has been an increased amount of attention paid to the phenomena of domestic violence. In relation to the probation service a number of areas have produced practice guidelines and strategies for working with both perpetrators and victims. The majority of these and other texts on the subject begin by providing a definition of the authors understanding of such violence. As different aspects of the perception of this problem have been incorporated these definitions have become more lengthy. Recently, some have begun to recognise the existence of domestic violence outside of a heterosexual relationship. What is disappointing however, is that the remainder of the discussions which follow fail to provide an account of this. Domestic violence within same-sex couples is considered to be an exception to the rule and not accorded a place in mainstream literature. The following attempts to start the rectification of this. Initially it was the author's intention to consider all same-sex couples. However, the differences which exist between gay and lesbian partnerships place such an analysis outside of the scope of this work. Lobel, 1986; Taylor and Chandler, 1995; Eaton, 1994 and Farley, 1992 all provide accounts of lesbian violence which may be useful. The material which directly addresses violence in gay male couples is more scarce.

Feminism, Heterosexism and Gay Male Domestic Violence

The majority of work which has influenced various agencies concerned with domestic violence has been clearly located within a tradition of feminist analysis of violence toward women from men. This analysis has been effective in terms of being able to pull together the links between women's oppression and the abuse or violence which many women suffer in their relationships with men. This perspective has become so prevalent that the subject of domestic abuse and violence has been considered to belong almost entirely to the area of feminist gender politics. It is commonly perceived that theories such as this operate within a paradigm of gender relations which create a barrier to alternative questions which as a result are never considered. This field therefore actively neglects an analysis of domestic violence which occurs in same-sex relationships. Specifically, all of the victims are female which in this context excludes the experience of gay men. In the rare works where the subject of same-sex violence is broached, it is usually referred to in terms of lesbian couples.

On a practical level those committed to working towards a reduction in the extent of domestic violence and the harm caused appear concerned that to accept the occurrence of domestic violence outside of relationships where men perpetrate violence against women, a dilution of women's experience will occur. These fears are acknowledged. However, attempts to have same-sex domestic violence recognised in no way seeks to compromise this position. By widening one's definition of domestic violence to include such abuse does not necessarily reduce the commitment to women abused by their male partners. It merely starts to recognise that some commitment needs to be made to those suffering violence in other relationships.

In cases where same-sex domestic violence has been considered, the directness of the challenge to heterosexist theory is not addressed. Domestic violence between lesbians or gay men has been referred to as an exception to the rule, or else is distorted to fit a space created by notions of gender politics. Twenty years ago, Martin (1976) claimed that violence occurs in relationships where same-sex partners act out masculine and feminine roles but is less likely to occur where such roles are not taken. Despite evidence that the vast majority of lesbians and gay men reject heterosexual roles for their relationships (Peplau, 1991) this view has been influential.

Estimates as to the extent of domestic violence within gay male relationships are anecdotal in nature. There has been no major empirical research conducted specifically targeting this question. From the USA, estimates include those from the Gay Men's Domestic Violence Project of the Community Against Violence in San Francisco. This states that 50 per cent of gay couples experience violence within their relationships. Island and Letellier (1991) believe that the figure is nearly proportionately double to that of heterosexual instances of violence. These are not accurate conclusions, but they are useful in placing the work into some context.

If radical feminist theory has contributed to the denial of violence within gay couples then it is clearly not appropriate to utilise such a framework to understand its occurrence. Gay men are not female. They do not possess that single quality which has been so far the focus of domestic violence theory. As Letellier (1994) states:

> *Sexism and misogyny cannot be the root cause of violence against these men. Their sexual orientation and gender may influence their reaction to the violence and their ability to escape from it, but they are not battered because they are men, nor because they are fulfilling a sex role stereotype.*

From a sociological perspective, authors have attended to structural and social factors which may have influence over the perpetration and occurrence of violence within relationships such as the extent to which social isolation performs a role within a persons experience of domestic violence (Neilsen *et al.*, 1992), and notions of cultural tolerance which allows violence to continue unchecked. Their findings would indicate that the relationship which exists between social isolation and battering is mutually dependant to some extent and that whilst battering precedes an increase in the isolation experienced by the battered partner, such isolation exists prior to the first incident of violence and apparently serves to create the conditions within which violence can occur through a lack of appropriate monitoring about the acceptability of such behaviour. This research, whilst influenced through notions of women in the home and the structural isolation created through the institution of marriage, can be of use outside of this framework and applied to the isolation experienced by gay couples from 'straight' society and gay communities. For gay men, this stance allows the consideration of the social context of homophobia and heterosexism within which domestic violence occurs. Further to this, the factors such as particular experiences of men as victims and the implications of this upon seeking help.

Of course, alone, socio-structural factors do not provide an adequate basis for understanding gay men's domestic violence. Psychological theories of relationships, violence, human development and mental illness are required to consider the individual differences between perpetrators (and to some extent their victims). A combination of these psychological and sociological approaches to the subject can account for victims and perpetrators of either gender. It does not necessarily reduce the experience of gay men to a heterosexist gender framework, yet acknowledges that such gender differences do exist and will form a basis for perceiving violence committed by men against female partners. There are likely similarities between heterosexual and gay male domestic violence. However, under this more inclusive model, gay relationships do not have to be treated as versions of heterosexual ones. Rather they are considered as men who have similar physical experiences of violence who will respond to and experience this in different ways.

The concept of power imbalance is closely entwined with definitions of domestic violence summarised as: *'Domestic violence involves the perpetration of violence by a more powerful person against a less powerful person.'* Such a conception however can be confusing and unsatisfactory. It is better expressed as an attempt to display or gain power by one person over another at a time when they feel that they do not possess such power. The notion is one of violence being perpetuated by an individual who believes themselves to be a 'non-person' and thereby insignificant.

Domestic violence between gay couples is still violence perpetrated by men. Questions of masculinity and violence are not new within this area. Instead of considering masculinity in terms of its relationship with women, understanding this violence requires consideration of masculinity for gay men. For gay males the confusion surrounding being masculine is compounded by a lack of visible gay role models. Pronger (1990) documents the links between masculinity, femininity, homosexuality and the cultural movements which have arisen from this. He postulates a dichotomy of gay roles being an effeminate 'camp' which initially arose as a response to notions of gay men being feminine and not real men. Later, there followed a reaction in the form of 'clone culture' within which ultra-masculine codes of dress and behaviour were exaggerated. The result of such a division of behaviour between masculine and feminine in the history of gay culture has led to a number of gay men having a complex and often confusing view of masculinity. Gondolf (1988, p4) describes male batterers as having a 'failed macho complex', and who see themselves as failing to reach the false masculine ideal of behaviour. They overcompensate for this by attempting to control the one who they perceive as threatening by being able to expose their insecurities, i.e. their lovers.

M. is a 29 year-old white male who was first brought to the attention of the probation service when a pre-sentence report was requested. He pleaded guilty to the offence of dangerous driving, having been stopped by the police. The pre-sentence report proposed a short probation order to consist of a drivers' group. Whilst M. may have benefitted from the information and work which he went through during the course of this probation order, it was not until the order was closing that the officer discovered that the male passenger in the car with M. was his partner. From this piece of information a wider picture of systematic violence alongside threats and intimidatory behaviour was formed. Driving dangerously was a frequent means by which M. contrived to intimidate and scare his partner.

The above case serves to show that the worker who seeks to understand the factors which are related to offending, needs to remain open minded about the possibility of domestic violence, and further, that the partner of the male client may be another man. How was this not picked up through supervision? There are a number of factors which may contribute to such homo-blindness and offer some explanation.

Invisible to Services
One obstacle which must be overcome is that of the inherent heterosexism which exists in many policies regarding domestic violence and the probation service. Such policies regard men who report that they are victims of

domestic violence to be themselves violent and should be worked with in that way:

Violence against men . . . is often retaliation for abuse by the man concerned. In work with males, therefore, it is necessary to address their treatment of the person who has harmed them.

This stance can therefore act as a barrier to effective working with the victims of gay male domestic violence who are not themselves violent. It is also contrary to other sections of domestic violence policies which urge probation workers to 'Recognise the victim's need for a positive response and your support.'

Each individual working relationship is constrained by the organisation within which it occurs. For example, within the probation service the inclusion of gay men and lesbians in equal opportunities statements is not universal practice, despite recommendations from NAPO, BASW, and CCETSW. Dunn (1996) postulates that:

. . . the law has so successfully criminalised gay relationships that Probation Committees find it hard to engage with the issue.   (Dunn, 1996, p65)

For agencies to progress toward adequate service delivery to the victims and perpetrators of gay male domestic violence, their approach to working with gay men generally must be considered. It may be a somewhat obvious point, but unless an open environment is created where clients feel able to express or consider their sexual identity, many workers will not be able to identify which of their clients are gay, bisexual or heterosexual, let alone which of those are involved in a violent gay relationship.

The probation service works with a large percentage of male offenders. This service is unable to fulfil its role of protecting the public effectively if it cannot engage with the proportion of these men who are gay. By avoiding the reality of an offender's sexuality, risk assessments become meaningless. One cannot assess the risks of offending and construct plans for effective supervision without some understanding of the context within which the offending occurs.

With specific reference to domestic violence, many of the essential guidelines for working with gay men are applicable. Workers need to have an awareness of the cultural diversity which exists between the gay and 'straight' community. As well as the diversity which exists within these communities. An important knowledge base is that of the process and effects of homophobia and heterosexism upon their gay client:

(Workers) who are ignorant of this discrimination cannot hope to engage meaningfully with gay (clients), and if they are unaware of the issues they

are unlikely to realise that someone they are supervising is gay. Dunn 1996, p66

This ignorance requires both challenge and addressing. The internal policies and procedures of any service may contribute to its heterosexist bias, and in order to make this service more accessible to gay, lesbian and bisexual clients they need to be reconsidered. Such a stance is important to rectify the damage and suspicion which many lesbians, gay men and bisexuals hold as a result of the legacy of many mental health and social work services defining homosexuality as a 'sin or sickness'.

Many workers will have absorbed the negative myths which surround the lifestyles of gay men and bring these alongside their personal cultural values into the relationships which they attempt to develop with clients. The individual characteristics and values of workers and clients form the basis of the relationships which develop. The homophobia and heterosexism of both need to be addressed. This process is not unique to heterosexual workers, processes of internalising oppression are discussed later which can apply equally to gay and lesbian workers. Each individual, regardless of sexual orientation and experience, will have their own beliefs and values surrounding the sexual behaviour of others.

Understanding the process of discrimination against gay men and recognising differences within the gay culture alone will not provide an adequate basis for non-heterosexist supervision. The effective worker must be able to draw links between the two. An increase in knowledge may simply serve to exacerbate a homophobic and judgmental stance towards a gay man's lifestyle. Dworkin and Gutiérrez (1989) note that people who are discriminated against develop strategies as a coping mechanism for this. Dunn (1996) clearly places lesbian and gay culture within the framework of these coping strategies, and urges workers to avoid judging or pathologising this culture according to the pertaining norms and expectations of heterosexuality.

In addition to homophobia's impact upon the services which exist, it can also play a part in preventing men affected by domestic violence in seeking help and dealing with the situation. This operates on a number of different levels but can be summarised within facets. Firstly, the ignorance of gay male domestic violence as a problem has prevented the construction of services and legislation for this group of men. Secondly, the fear of having their relationship even further invalidated prevents many gay men from seeking help concerning a problem within it or with one of the partners. One survivor of domestic violence quoted in Lobel (1986) states:

None of us ever sought professional counselling out of fear that our lifestyle would be revealed and that any therapist would view homosexuality as 'the problem'. (Lobel, 1986, p37)

This points to the inheritance from the behavioural sciences and related professions which view homosexuality as a disorder. However, such invalidation can be felt from family and friends and therefore serves to perpetuate the hidden nature of this violence.

Within the case example shown at the beginning of this section it is, of course within the interests of M. to keep this violence hidden. By not engaging with the issue of sexuality a grossly inadequate risk assessment was formed. M., being aware that the probation officer is not informed as to the nature of his relationship with the passenger in his car, is able to continue to present himself a willing participant in supervision which presents no challenge to the causes of his offending, and no long term protection for his partner and victim.

Invisible to Society

Many gay couples are isolated from friends and family as a result of intolerance and homophobia (Sanderson, 1994). In the wider community, gay relationships are not validated through legal means, such as Section 28 of the Local Government Act 1988 and the unequal ages of consent for gay men and heterosexuals.

The majority of validated heterosexual relationships have certain rites of passage which are marked by celebrations such as engagements, weddings, birth of children etc. With no such markers the gay couple are forced to depend much more upon each other for support. The effects of this, and the more general social opprobrium which society places upon gay couples, can be that the two become much more dependant upon one another (Masters and Johnson, 1979). Precursors which can create the conditions for violence within relationships are stresses and social isolation which the couple are experiencing (Schupe *et al.*, 1987, pp28–33). The examples which they cite are those of finances, careers and responsibilities. Institutional heterosexism and a lack of anti-discrimination legislation on the grounds of sexual orientation exists particularly within the realms of employment and housing. Pension rights are rarely passed on to the partner if they are of the same sex, benefits which are given to married couples do not apply within gay relationships and there is no legislation to protect the gay couple from eviction by a landlord simply because they are gay. If these areas of heterosexual couples' lives are stressful, then it is probable that given the added strain of isolation and invalidation placed upon gay relationships these couples will find such points more stressful and thus a more effective precursor to violence.

Invisible to Victims

One of the unique characteristics of gay male battering is that many gay men are unable to see that they are victims of this form of violence simply because they are men. Letellier (1994) states that many of the gay men he has worked with view battering within a relationship as something which only happens to women. Seeking help is affected as this act reinforces the sense of failure which they experience not only as a partner in a violent relationship but also as a man (McMullen, 1990). The notion of men as victims does not sit comfortably with our inheritance of victimology.

Our culture provides no room for a man as victim. Men are simply not supposed to be victimised. A 'real man' is expected to be able to protect himself in any situation. He is supposed to be able to solve any problem and recover from any set-back. (Lew 1988, p41)

Given the above, it is likely that many gay men are unable to characterise what is happening to them in a relationship as domestic violence. As a result, they may not take the necessary emotional or practical steps to deal with the situation. This is likely particularly at the early stages of the violence before the cycles of violence are in motion and they find that they are not able to get out.

Hunter's (1990) discussion about male incest survivors claims that they do not conceptualise their situation and experiences as abuse. Their notions of victimisation are not ones which sit comfortably with their male identity and as a result do not allow themselves to be given the label of victim. Evans' (1990) study of male sexual assault survivors showed that for a man a high level of physical effects of trauma and injury must be present in order to validate his internal reactions to the event. In other words, if a man is not severely injured he will not be able to see himself as victimised in a situation:

The common psychological reactions to violence, such as fear, vulnerability, shock, and depression, in the absence of a black eye, a fractured rib, or a stab wound, may not be sufficient for the man to associate his experience with the concept of victimisation. (Letellier 1994, p99)

Such perceptions of men as victims fits clearly within the situation of gay men who suffer from the violence of their partners. Snow (1992) writing for *The Advocate* about same-sex domestic violence quoted a social worker on the subject of working with a gay man who had been beaten by his lover for almost ten years:

After being assaulted with a lead pipe and almost killed . . . this man was still able to seriously ask the question, 'Well, do you really think that was domestic violence?'. (Snow 1992, p61)

One can postulate that many of the gay men who suffer from abuse are unable to make this known to agencies who may be able to assist. Those men are unlikely to be able to describe their situation as domestic violence, even to themselves, and so are not aware that there really is a problem, or potential problem. Secondly, as male 'problem solvers' they are much less likely to tell anyone about the abuse and less likely to seek help. Through this situation these men are in a position of greater risk of further violence and abuse. In addition to problems within services described earlier, this impacts upon those men who have reached a point of acknowledging the need for intervention. Having got this far, services then fail them.

Principles of working with male domestic violence victims or survivors remain the same. These include the belief that they are telling the truth about the violence which they experience. It was shown how men's experience of victimisation often requires greater physical injury than that of women. Should a gay male victim of domestic violence disclose this violence, he will need to be taken seriously. Risking rejection by disclosing his sexuality and presenting himself as a male victim in a culture which does not easily accept either of these, it is unlikely that he is not telling the truth.

The victims own experience of the violence should be validated however, any notion that he is to blame for the violence must be rejected. Many victims of anti-gay violence feel that they deserve their injuries because they are gay (Bohn, 1984). Colgan (1987) found that amongst gay counselling clients there was a pattern of reacting to accumulative rejections by others with self-blame. There is a difficult balance which must be achieved between examining the behaviour of the victim in the context of the violent relationship, whilst not making the victim feel responsible for the violence.

Victims of abuse are also likely to be unable to acknowledge their victim status through the confusion which surrounds their actions during the violence. The actions of the victim do have some sequential truth to them e.g. if they had not refused to leave a party when their partner wanted to then there would not have been a dispute about it. However, there is no objective truth here. That is to say, despite the clear role played by the victim in the incident it is not his fault that the result of the dispute was violence meted out to him. This may seem rather obvious yet for some victims it is possible to intellectually accept this and have a strong desire not to feel at fault but not actually feel exonerated from blame.

The role which the victim plays within the violence cannot, nevertheless, be ignored. The victim must be able to take responsibility for their choices to extricate themselves from the abuse. Should the perpetrator want to stop the violence, then the victim must make the choice between leaving the relationship or staying and working with the violence. Above all, the worker must challenge the statements of the victim which encourage helplessness.

Supporting the victim role may be why survivors often go back into the same or another abusive relationship. (Farley, 1992, p241)

Towards Understanding Gay Male Domestic Violence

Much progress has been made by organisations fighting for respect and rights to be awarded to gay men and lesbians, over the past two decades, since the famous Stonewall incident in the late 1960s. Despite this, lesbians, gay men and bisexuals are continually subjected to homophobia. This homophobia takes many forms from anti-gay physical and verbal violence through to legal, educational and other institutional forms of discrimination and oppression against gay men and women.

The many forms which homophobia takes in modern society has been documented elsewhere. Here it is more fruitful to consider the effects of this homophobia on individual gay men and on the relationships which they enter into. With respect to violence within these relationships there are two main ways in which violent gay relationships are affected. We have already considered how the social context of homophobia can prevent those experiencing domestic violence from seeking help. Further though, some understanding is needed of the individual gay man's response to the knowledge that he develops within a society which continually reminds him of his difference.

Despite the fact that research indicates that the majority of gay men are as mentally healthy as heterosexuals, it is not surprising that many gay men find difficulty in maintaining feelings of self worth and dignity (Isay, 1989). The sense of difference felt by gay men can be interpreted as 'being defective'. This is backed up by much writing and research on the subject of homosexuality. West (1987) sums up the conclusions of this 'homosexuality as an illness' perspective when he states that 'bisexuals and homosexuals are life's neurotic failures.' (p99).

The existence of AIDS is a further dimension which affects the psychological lives of many gay men in a particular way. The politics of AIDS and its links with the gay community has led to the fact that 'some healthy young adults now perceive themselves as potential carriers of death' (Isay, 1989, p68). Odets (1990) discusses this point with reference to more general homophobia:

The homosexual man, often considered psychologically 'sick' for his sexuality, and who homophobically concurs with this conclusion, is now sick with AIDS, an apparent physical validation of the moral and psychological judgements against homosexuals. (Odets, 1990, p1)

Such internalised homophobia was so prevalent in Odet's research that many of the men which he encountered in the course of the study were more comfortable with their identity as people living with AIDS than with their identity as gay men.

The resulting low self-esteem from this may contribute to a poor ability to develop committed and trusting relationships. Further effects of this can be that the gay man turns the feeling of worthlessness into a hatred of those parts of himself and others. The process of internalising the oppression against gay men can become acted out in horizontal hostility, an expression of self-hatred felt owing to one's membership of a minority group. Instead of showing hostility toward the oppressing force it is safer to direct this against other people (Pharr, 1988). Structurally, this horizontal hostility can be viewed as the oppression of other groups by minority groups. On a more individual level this can lead to being unwilling to psychologically identify with other members of one's own oppressed group and developing a clearer link to those who serve to oppress. e.g. gay men expressing hostility toward other gay men. Sanderson (1994) describes working with a gay man being counselled for his self-hatred. In the process of this counselling he states:

> *I realised after a while I always begin to feel a bit contemptuous of the men I meet. It was a strange thing really, but however pleasant they were and however much I liked them, I kept thinking they were inferior, not like real men* ... (Sanderson, 1994, p18)

When inside a relationship the gay man who feels this has a difficult construction of self to maintain. The formation of a healthy gay identity can be characterised as a process of different stages (Cass, 1979; Ford, 1993). Prior to the individual becoming fully integrated into an acceptance of himself as a gay man the defining characteristics of his gayness is in terms of the actions which he performs. The partner of such a gay man therefore becomes the primary defining feature of his gay lifestyle and the primary target for hatred and disgust. As a gay man, he has developed a relationship to fulfil his emotional and sexual needs, yet identifying with the heterosexual 'straight' world he finds this distasteful at times.

The overwhelming feeling is one of being out of control. It is not difficult to see how it is easier for this man to blame his partner for this situation as his partner becomes the defining feature of his gay lifestyle and at the same time the primary object of resentment and self-hatred. The links from this situation to domestic violence are not difficult to construct. In this situation one partner has a sense of not being in control and is clearly able to identify one person to whom the blame for this can be attributed. Whilst violence is certainly not inevitable, given what we already know it is unsurprising that some men respond to this in abusive ways toward their partner. In attempting to understand the role which violence specifically plays within this, the Duluth, Minnesota model of abuse and violence within relationships may be of assistance. It is not necessarily the case that the perpetrator of abuse moves immediately from a position of feeling uncertain about his situation to that of violence, rather that violence is one, extreme means by which the perpetrator seeks to exert his control over the relationship. Transferring his own oppression onto his partner creates dissonance within the perpetrator. Uncomfortable about this, it is perceived by him to be his responsibility to address this dissonance, although not through addressing his own problems but through forcing his partner to act in other ways and to 'become something different.' It is when other forms of abuse fail to achieve this that violence is used.

An adequate assessment of the offending will determine the effectiveness of the supervision which follows. The challenge for the probation worker is turning these theories into practice which seeks to assist offenders to adjust from using violence within a relationship to behaving non-violently. In working with gay male perpetrators of domestic violence there are two emphases which can be placed upon the work. The offender can be regarded as a gay man who is violent, or as a violent man who is gay. The effects of this differing emphasis are to shape the outline and content of the supervision.

A gay man who is violent

This assessment is based upon the belief that it is the homophobia and consequences of this internalisation of oppression which is of fundamental importance to the resulting violent behaviour. Constructing supervision for working with this involves 'gay affirmation' (Morin, 1991). Such an approach seeks to remove the stigma which has been associated with a homosexual identity and includes personal and political perspectives to enable the client to recognise the normality of his identity. Of course, this work alone will not achieve the aim of enabling the violent client to respond in appropriate ways to his partner. However, it is important groundwork which needs priority.

A violent man who is gay

The role of homophobia is clearly a large one, but this is not to claim that all gay men react in the same way and that these are inevitable difficulties. Nevertheless, this does provide an account of the specific experiences of gay men which separate them out from heterosexual men who use violence. In some instances the reasons for the violence may be the same. In other cases, the reasons may be clearly located within the above framework. Likewise, it is not the intention of this to present an impression that the difficulties faced by gay men through homophobia are always resolved through violence and hatred.

The underlying factors of gay male domestic violence discussed earlier are by no means an exhaustive account. It may be the case that the violence is much more concerned with male attitudes and behaviour choices which have more in common with the perpetration of violence generally. In these instances, affirmative counselling is not appropriate and merely serves to obfuscate the more basic problem of violence. It is still important to note however, that the gay identity of the client cannot be ignored and should be discussed in the context of the effects of the violence upon the client and the victim:

> *Even though the concerns may be no different, the issues are exacerbated by the ignorance, prejudice, oppression, and homophobia that gays and lesbians must address.* (House and Holloway, 1992, pp308–309)

Domestic violence is often considered to be a difficult and complex area for probation workers to become deeply involved with during supervision. Given the difficulties of this and the demands of large workloads it is understandable that groupwork programmes (where they exist) are popular for purely practical purposes outside of any particular successes and effectiveness which they provide. Despite the similarities which may exist between the gay male and the heterosexual male in his violent behaviour, the different experiences of sexual identity render a mixed group setting inappropriate and demand that work with gay males on violence be conducted within individual supervision (until groups can be run for gay men).

Conclusion

It can be seen how the progress which has been made toward understanding and working with the violence men use against women has stood in the way of exploring the violence used within same-sex and particularly male couples. It is only by returning to basic notions of acceptance of individuals and their accounts of their experiences that we can hope to engage with them on the deeper levels that working with domestic violence requires.

While discussing the history of domestic violence work, Schupe *et al.* (1987) provides four reasons for optimism about its future. They list these as: an increase in public awareness; an increase in political awareness; legal changes; and research. At the present time, it appears that there is still an uphill struggle facing those who wish to see domestic violence between gay male couples addressed satisfactorily.

In order for workers to fully understand the dynamics within gay relationships and the violence which occurs, specific research needs to be conducted. The arguments presented here are in need of empirical analysis. Until this occurs, it is up to individuals and services to adopt anti-heterosexist ways of working which may enable them to understand the particular circumstances of their client, the context of offending and then construct effective supervision which reduces future risks.

References

Bohn, T.R. (1984) *Homophobic Violence: Implications for Social Work Practice*. New York: Haworth.

Cass, V. (1979) Homosexual Identity Formation: A Theoretical Model. *Journal of Homosexuality*. 4(3) pp219–235.

Colgan, P. (1987) Assessment of Sexual Orientation. *Journal of Homosexuality*. 4 pp219–236.

Dunn, P. (1996) Sexuality: Is There a Hierarchy of Discrimination? *Probation Journal*. 43(2). pp64–70.

Dworkin, S.H. and Gutiérrez, F. (1989) Counsellors be Aware: Clients Come in Every Size, Shape, Colour, and Sexual Orientation. *Journal of Counselling and Development*. 68(1) pp6–8.

Eaton, M. (1994) Abuse by Any Other Name: Feminism, Difference and Intra-lesbian Violence. In Fineman, M.A. and Mykitiuk, R. (Eds), *The Public Nature of Private Violence: The Discovery of Domestic Abuse*. London: Routledge.

Evans, P. (1990) The Needs of the Blue-eyed Arab: Crisis Intervention with Male Sexual Assault Survivors. In Hunter, M. (Ed.), *The Sexually Abused Male: Prevalence, Impact and Treatment*. Toronto: Lexicon Books. pp193–225.

Farley, N. (1992) Same-sex Domestic Violence. In Dworkin, S.H. and Gutiérrez, F. *Counseling Gay Men and Lesbians: Journey to the End of the Rainbow*. Alexandria, Va: American Counseling Association.

Ford, R. (1993) *Gay Identity and Probation Practice*. Unpublished MA thesis. UEA: Norwich.

Gondolf, E.W. (1988) *Research on Men Who Batter: An Overview, Bibliography and Resource Guide*. Bradenton, Florida, Human Services Institute.

House, R.M., and Holloway, E.L. (1992) Empowering the Counseling Professional to Work with Lesbian and Gay Issues. In Dworkin, S.H. and Gutiérrez,F. *Counseling Gay Men and Lesbians: Journey to the End of the Rainbow*. Alexandria, Va: American Counseling Association.

Hunter, M. (1990) *Abused Boys: The Neglected Victims of Sexual Abuse*. New York: Fawcett Columbine.

Isay, R.A. (1989) *Being Homosexual: Gay Men and their Development*. London: Penguin.

Island, D. and Letellier, P. (1991) *Men Who Beat the Men Who Love Them*. Binghamton, NY: Harington Park Press.

Letellier, P. (1994) Gay and Bisexual Male Domestic Violence Victimization: Challenges to Feminist Theory and Responses to Violence. *Violence and Victims*. 9(2) pp95–106.

Lew, M. (1988) *Victims no Longer: Men Recovering from Incest and Other Child Abuse*. New York: Harper & Row.

Lobel, K. (Ed.) (1986) *Naming the Violence: Speaking out Against Lesbian Battering*. Seattle: Seal Press.

Martin, D. (1976) *Battered Wives*. New York: Simon and Schuster.

Masters, W.H. and Johnson, V.E. (1979) *Homosexuality in Perspective*. Boston: Little Brown.

McMullen, R.J. (1990) *Male Rape: Breaking the Silence on the Last Taboo*. London: GMP Publishers.

Morin, S.F. (1991) Removing the Stigma: Lesbian and Gay Affirmative Counseling. *The Counseling Psychologist* 19(2) pp245–247.

Nielsen, J.M., Endo, R.K. and Ellington, B.L. (1992) Social Isolation and Wife Abuse: A Research Report. In Viano, E.C. (Ed.), *Intimate Violence: Interdisciplinary Perspectives*. (pp49–60) Bristol, PA: Taylor & Francis.

Odets, W. (1990) *The Homosexualization of AIDS. Focus: A Guide to AIDS Research and Counselling*. 5 pp1–2.

Peplau, L.A. (1991) Lesbian and Gay Relationships. In Gonsiorek, J.C. and Weinrich, J.D. (Eds) *Homosexuality: Implications for Public Policy*. pp177–196 Newbury Park, California: Sage Publications.

Pharr, S. (1988) *Homophobia: A Weapon of Sexism*. Little Rock: Chardon Press.

Pronger, B. (1990) *The Arena of Masculinity: Sports, Homosexuality and the Meaning of Sex*. London: Gay Men's Press.

Sanderson, T. (1994) *Making Gay Relationships Work: A Handbook for Male Couples*. London: The Other Way Press.

Schupe, A., Stacey, W.A. and Hazlewood, L.R. (1987) *Violent Men, Violent Couples: The Dynamics of Domestic Violence*. Lexington, Mass: Lexington Books.

Snow, K. (1992) The Violence at Home. *The Advocate*. June 2nd. pp60–64.

Taylor, J. and Chandler, T. (1995) *Lesbians Talk Violent Relationships*. London: Scarlett Press.

West, D.J. (1987) *Sexual Crimes and Confrontations*. Aldershot: Gower.

CHAPTER 8

Transpeople: Working with Gender Dysphoria

Leonie Williams and David Phillips

Introduction

Any person who wishes to dispute the importance of gender and sexuality in society only has to explore the position of transpeople within it. Instead of giving those citizens who believe that their birth gender was wrongly assigned (whatever the physical 'evidence' to the contrary), support, advice and help, it subjects them to ridicule, disbelief and silence. We would suggest that only a society which uses sexuality and gender in its power relations would function so. As authors, we do not intend to provide a detailed medical/social analysis of why transpeople exist, although the provision of some information will be necessary. Instead, we write from the standpoint that transpeople exist and have a right to do so. We hope to account for the difficulties we had as probation officers working with transpeople who were also offenders, and how the lack of information and the prejudice that we experienced alongside them made our job and their lives so much harder. We hope thus to provide some insights for other professionals.

The job of a probation officer could be summarised as assessing the risk that offenders present to society and working with them to reduce that risk. Thus a clear head, and an ability to focus on this without the taint of stereotypes is highly significant. We would acknowledge that the first time we were each individually presented with the notion of working with an offender who was either considering, or going through, the 'sex change' process, we felt curiosity and panic, swiftly followed by fear. We were 'out of our depth'. We had access to little or no knowledge from our professional training and little sense of where to go to get it.

Now several years on, we would not describe ourselves as 'specialists', but as two practitioners who have worked with people going through the transgender process, who were also offenders and therefore under the scrutiny of the criminal justice system. We would like to share the information and understanding we gained and the dilemmas we still do not feel are resolved with other practitioners. By so doing we hope the results will be a more informed and secure base for others to work from and a better and more sensitive service to transgender people.

The people we worked with were transgender people and they were also offenders. This brought some particular dilemmas of its own, described later.

Perhaps the central one, for us, was to focus on the need to judge the risk of harm and re-offending that is integral to Probation Practice. There was, first of all, an over-reaction to transpeople, they must be dangerous, because they are what they are. This involved us in a great deal of examination of our personal feelings. Secondly, the basis of all risk assessment is information gathering, and it was therefore imperative to understand some of the specific experiences of transpeople when completing a risk assessment. Thus our knowledge base had to expand. Thirdly, however, we defined that the demands of the criminal law process, the impact of counselling, medical help or treatment or simply the search for access or funding for this, could be so overwhelming for the individual as to completely marginalise our concerns for them. We had to be very clear that probation officers are not there to provide a route to medical services, nor counselling about the transgender experience. We maintained our own agendas, but, to work from a position of ensuring that the person was treated with equality, we had to take their experience of pain or surgery or humiliation constantly into account. Finally, it was only too easy for us to be seen as experts, which we are not, and consequently dumped on by colleagues. We would suggest co-working may help practitioners to handle some of these dilemmas better, as could the introduction of a better training base during and after qualification.

Working with offenders throws up many issues and well rehearsed discussions with regards to social control, labelling, deviance, or nature verses nurture. Most of these debates, however heated, take assigned gender as a constant. Working with people who feel they have been designated the wrong gender at birth therefore adds an additional complicated and confusing dimension. We hope that our experience gained in a probation setting will provide a framework useful to discussions in other disciplines.

Important Definitions

This chapter uses the following definitions:

A transsexual person is any person who believes they have been designated the wrong gender at birth. The issues around designated birth gender are discussed more fully later in the chapter.

An offender is a person whose behaviour has resulted in them being dealt with by the criminal courts.

Distinction must be made between the terms gender, sexuality, and sexual acts, as a basis for understanding transsexuality.

'Gender' is the social construct of the way a person lives their life, and is perceived by others.

Sexuality is the way someone feels about themselves, and also how they are attracted to others. That attraction may manifest itself as physical acts, or fantasies, or a combination of the two.

Sexual acts are self-explanatory but do not necessarily define sexuality, indeed it is possible for people to use sexual acts to either deny or distract attention from their sexuality. Every individuals understanding of sexuality will be personal to them, but possibly different to that of others. Sexuality can also fluctuate throughout a person's life.

Transsexuality and Offending

Textbooks account for the customary influences and factors in an offenders life at the time of offending (e.g., relationship breakdown, homelessness or substance abuse). The offender who is at any point in the transsexual process is subject to those same experiences. In addition, they may be dealing with a variety of inner confusions, anger at the process they are going through and anxiety about its outcomes. Offending is not necessarily linked to the transsexual process as such and transsexuality may or may not be relative for risk assessment and analysis. Conversely, that means that just because someone is transsexual this does not mean that they pose a risk. The task for the probation officer is to assess just how much what the person is going through has affected their behaviour and how much it will continue to do so. Since the stereotypical view of the transsexual is of someone who at best is very sick and confused, and at worst some kind of monster, clarity of thought is not easy to come by.

By the time they come into contact with a probation officer, transpeople are likely to have a substantial experience of the criminal justice system or of other professionals.

They are likely to have experienced substantial prejudice and ignorance, and their attitude to the worker may well vary from complete dismissal on the one hand, to perceiving the worker as their advocate, saviour, and emotional sponge on the other.

The practitioner is faced with new and sometimes frightening feelings. Fear of getting it wrong, lack of knowledge and understanding, and personal prejudices which change as the process progresses. It is all too easy to completely lose focus. From our experiences, both working separately and together with transpeople, we have found ourselves overwhelmed by issues of diagnosis, seeking treatment and funding, and adjustments to changing social experiences. We have only later realised that we have totally forgotten 'offending behaviour'. Even when trying to plan work on offending, it is very difficult to maintain the line of personal responsibility of the offender when the practitioner is drawn into the whirlpool of social, medical and political forces which the offender is experiencing.

The conclusion we draw from these considerations is that there is a need for a clear programme of intervention with defined aims and objectives looking towards thinking skills or direct, offence based programmes of work. In addition, throughout contact, time also needs to be built in but clearly set aside from offender based work, to consider the needs of the offender and to provide advice, support and advocacy. This needs to remain high profile so that one set of considerations does not overwhelm another. Co-working or having different people offer each piece of work may help.

Understanding the Daily Experience

Some of the difficulties of carrying on a life throughout the transgender process should be obvious. Moving around in society dressed as the 'opposite' gender to the one that people have known before evokes an often negative response that the very term 'opposite' suggests.

That apparently simple statement conceals other pitfalls. There is the cost of completely replacing a wardrobe, not just once, but on a continual basis as the body shape changes. In practice, buying clothes, using public toilets and accessing gender specific resources can be a nightmare, underlined always by the dichotomy between presenting as the 'opposite' gender but living with all the official documents and means of identification remaining in the birth gender. Other complex issues are soon apparent, such as a breakdown in communication with parents and family who either do not know what their kin are going through, or do not understand. If families do not know, the person will fear rejection if the truth is out. If they do know, predictable reactions are fear, anger, and grief at the loss of their 'son' or 'daughter', 'brother' or 'sister'.

If understanding is clear from a young age, a child may become introverted and isolated if they believe they are the only one who feels this way. Such feelings can lead to problems at school, school phobia or behaving in a hyper female or macho way. Some adults marry and have either unsuccessful sexual relationships with their partners, or produce children before inner conflict forces them to face up to their need to change. This process will also be familiar to gay men and lesbian women, and it indicates how strong is the indoctrination to present as a stereotypical, heterosexual version of the gender assigned you at birth, however uncomfortable that is socially and psychologically.

Making a Change

When transpeople have made a personal decision that they have a need for change, the process is long, frustrating, uncomfortable and at times painful. Talking to the right people, getting appropriate practical, medical, and psychiatric advice is far from easy, and when accessed is often provided without a supportive environment.

With the help of an understanding general practitioner a person can begin the process which involves being seen by two psychiatrists who must both agree that the process is appropriate for this person at this time. The person then has to live as the opposite birth gender for up to two years, taking long-term hormone treatment which can be administered orally or by injections, and often going through voice therapy and electrolysis to remove unwanted body hair. Finally, surgery, which even if welcomed can be extensive and invasive, with all the exhaustion, emotional turmoil and post-operative concerns of any major surgery. All of this, of course, is subject to any individual successfully seeking health service funds or finding some private means to pay.

It is relatively clear to see how such personal pressures might trigger or exacerbate the potential for substance misuse, or mental health problems such as depression. Equally, financial problems can lead to dishonesty offences, whilst anger and resentment towards self and society can lead to offences of violence to the self or others. In all of these situations the transperson is not just a transperson but a human being subject to a whole range of other constraints and exhibiting a whole range of skills.

Other social work professionals could well be involved as a result of the decisions to change assigned gender. Family court welfare officers, for example, can find themselves dealing with contact and residence applications in relation to families torn apart by the decision and by the confusion and prejudice of other family members. Social workers may find themselves dealing with accusations of child abuse. The difficulty that all these professionals face is the difficulty we faced, a lack of access to knowledge with which to combat one's own and others prejudices.

We have tried in the rest of this chapter to provide enough practical and informative knowledge on a 'need to know' basis to fellow practitioners, using the following headings for ease of access:

- philosophy
- designating sexuality
- terminology
- issues for clients and for practitioners
- issues for institutions
- transsexual prisoners and housing
- the law and employment
- funding
- the medical view
- conclusion

It is not possible to give complete information on medical, legal and political issues and, of course, the situation changes constantly. References and a list of resources to enable further research are provided at the end of the chapter.

Philosophy

Underpinning all professional work there should be a definition of a person's human rights, especially within the context of gender and sexuality. Rothblatt has listed a number of points from the Gender Bill of Rights. In essence, these may be summarised as ensuring an individual's right to define identity and acknowledging that:

> *All human beings carry within themselves an ever-unfolding idea of who they are and what they are capable of achieving. An individual's identity and capability cannot be circumscribed by what society deems to be masculine or feminine behaviour.*

The International Bill of Gender Rights was approved and adopted by the Second International Conference on Transgender Law and Employment Policy, August 28th, 1993, in Houston, Texas.

Designating Sexuality

There are thought to be 25,000 transsexuals within the UK. Of these, some 60 per cent are transsexual to female, and some 40 per cent are transsexual to male. Gerard Greaves in his article *I am never going to be a man mummy* (Express 26.10.97) says that up to 600 children, some as young as seven, are leading lives as transsexuals after being diagnosed as having a rare psychological condition and that psychiatrists report that numbers are rising every year as awareness increases. (This article was reproduced in Press for Change release McNab 1.11.97)

Another article, in *The Observer* newspaper, designated this condition as intersex and said that it affects 1 child in 12,000 or about 60 births in Britain each year. The article claims that a rare hormonal imbalance during pregnancy causes the 'condition'. It is worth noting here that O'Keefe and Fox (1997) devote a whole chapter to possible causes and the many theories which abound. *The Observer* article also commented on the difficulties of designating babies' sex at birth. In the case of intersex 'the shape of the genitals becomes indeterminate. The child possesses a tiny penis or an enlarged clitoris, and in these circumstances it is fiendishly difficult to be certain in which gender the new arrival belongs' (Observer 1.3.98). At Great Ormond Street Hospital a team of doctors attempt to decide on gender within the first year. A Suffolk Health Authority report (1994) quotes from an unspecified 1974 report, that the prevalence of transsexualism was estimated at 1 in 34,000 males and at 1 in 108,000 females, a male to female ratio of about 3:1 (Suffolk H.A., 1994). Those figures are also reflected in the *Advisory Bulletin on Employment Relations* (March 1998) which quotes an estimate of 1 in *30,000* men and 1 in *100,000* women as experiencing transsexualism. It is worth noting that these figures are estimates, and probably underestimate the true numbers. It is also stressed in a GDTI (Gender Dysphoria Trust International) booklet that *a transsexual can be a heterosexual person who may have been married and raised a family.* 'Transexuality is not homosexuality and the desire to change ones ascribed gender exists independently of choice of sexuality both before and after the change has occurred' (GDTI 1992). A government consultation paper produced by the Department of Education and Employment provoked an angry response from the 'Press for Change' campaigning group. One of the chief objections to the policy was that it seemed to limit the professions in which transpeople could be employed by preventing them from working with people under the age of 18 or in professions involving contact with members of the public. Spokeswoman Christine Burns commented that 'This paper isn't about protecting us from society. It seems to be about protecting society from us.' (Press for Change, Feb., 1998)

Under British law, gender designation once decided is fixed for life, so even after a person has undergone the extensive physical and mental processes required and become effectively a different gender, their legal status remains unchanged. Struggles against this continue with some victories. A transperson who changed from male to female was barred from a Nottingham Women's Centre, although after discussion and lobbying the policy was changed to permit access to transpeople. (*Nottingham Evening Post* 30.4.98) More negatively, the Court of Human Rights in Strasbourg in July, 1998 rejected an appeal by two British transpeople to change their birth certificates. There are only a few countries remaining (who are signatories to the Convention of Human Rights) who refuse this re-registering: one is Britain, the others are Ireland, Andorra and Albania.

Terminology

An understanding of the following terms is necessary when discussing transsexualism and transpeople:

sex/gender	All the characteristics which distinguish organisms on the basis of reproductive function.
gender/identity	Social construct of gender.
sex change	A process by which an organism changes from male to female or female to male.
transsexual	One who may begin life as one biological sex, then implements a self-motivated, complete transformation to appear and behave as another sex.
transsexualism	A strong desire to change sex.

gender dysphoria	A persistent discomfort with one's sex or gender.
gender identity disorder	As above
transvestite	Wearing clothes traditionally considered to be of the opposite sex.
hermaphrodite	A true hermaphrodite is someone who is born with organs attributed to both sexes. A pseudo-hermaphrodite (female) is a female who shows secondary male characteristics (virilism) possibly mental or physical.
psychosexual genetics	Is the study of genetic formulations that bear upon the psychosexual behaviour patterns whenever they are determined.

(O'Keefe and Fox, 1997)

It is our experience that understanding and acceptance of sexuality is fluid. Sexual attraction, for example, may change and vary from time to time, depending on the individuals and their experiences at any given time. As workers, we need to be sensitive to people's sexuality and not make assumptions or attempt to impose labels. In relation to transpeople it can be as damaging to put gay stereotypes onto them as it is to impose straight stereotypes. Transsexuality is not homosexuality, though the two groups may experience commonly based prejudices. A presumption that male to female transsexuality creates a person who is homosexual is erroneous.

Issues for Clients and Practitioners

Probation officers may encounter transpeople in a variety of settings within the community and within custodial institutions. It may be that they have colleagues going through the transsexual process. Other professionals will also find themselves, knowingly or otherwise, offering their services to transsexuals.

Just as 'coming out' for gay and lesbian people is difficult, acknowledging transsexuality and dealing with it is as intensive a struggle. There are comparable issues about who to tell and when, together with the individuals own insecurity and perhaps uncertainty. The fear of other people's negative reactions which predictably include disbelief, horror, and ridicule inhibit disclosure. To gay and lesbian people such considerations may be obvious from their own experience, but the explanation perhaps needs to be made to all colleagues who have contact with transpeople. There is 'furthermore' a body of knowledge about gays and lesbians which does not exist for transsexuals. It says a lot about the oppression within society that no-one seems to expect reaction to be favourable. In our experience the most people hope for is a neutral non-judgmental response. Of course this is an area where support is essential from professional workers and access to other transpeople vital.

There may be critical points in a person's life where sensitivity to the issues is vital for workers as for example those who deal with youth:

The point at which a young teenage person may coherently incorporate their transsexualism into their life plan may be a time when childhood fades and the cruel realities of shaping their own lives present them with a very narrow set of alternatives. (O'Keefe and Fox, 1997)

At all times however, it is important for workers to be aware of terminology, and support networks, and to be able to give information and contact telephone numbers to individuals. We suggest they should be displayed on notice boards in all offices and regrettably, monitored for graffiti.

Issues for Institutions

As with work in the community, there is a role for direct advocacy, but within the prison system, it is again necessary for probation officers to separate advocacy from the responsibility of protecting the public from offenders. Thus a prisoner who may identify gender dysphoria as an overriding issue must not be allowed to lose sight of their offending behaviour and its consequences for others. It is, again, our experience that it is easy to focus on the issue of transsexualism to the exclusion of all other issues, and it therefore becomes more difficult to make accurate risk assessments. For example, when working with transpeople who are serving long or life sentences, the question of using the transgender process as a manipulative 'way out of prison' has to be considered. Is this person genuinely transsexual, or do they believe going through this process will reduce the authority's perception of them as a risk? If, as professionals, we are to accept the need to validate a persons self declared sexuality, how do we reconcile this dilemma? The authors believe that better risk assessments, based on well researched information, can be completed, as long as consideration is given to the issues discussed above.

For transpeople within custody there are immediate issues which need to be addressed. Institutions work on the principle of management by gender division and the pretence that sexuality is consequently not an issue (Barter, 1997) and so the location of transsexuals presents an immediate problem. For example, a man who wishes to become a woman will be confined to a male prison. If his description of his sexuality is not accepted then he may not even be accorded the safety of the hospital wing. If he is accepted as a transsexual and allowed to wear women's clothes, we wonder whether this a true measure of living life as a woman within the very male community where female contact is minimal and cannot by its nature be on an equal power basis. If transferred to a women's prison the experience may be equally unhelpful. The opportunity to move around in open society and learn to live as a woman in that society is denied to that person. Therefore risk assessments made pre-release are based on an unreal assumption.

Prisoners are no less likely than the general public to openly express prejudice and discrimination. O'Keefe and Fox (1997) referring to a Canadian study by Maxine Peterson on the rights of transsexuals in prison reported that, conditions varied between different countries but rape, beatings, constant mental abuse and even murder were common. They concluded that it is extremely difficult for many transsexuals to survive oppressive inhumane regimes and often these people become socio-economic victims forced into crime. They found this indicative of the way many cultures actually see transsexualism itself, as a moral and legal crime.

We know of a case of a serving prisoner where an initial decision to prescribe HRT and provide other facilities such as elocution lessons, while the offender was serving a sentence, began the process of medical re-assignment and responsibility for funding. However, authorities do not routinely make funds available for surgery to complete the process, neither do they fund appropriate medical care. In the case we have cited, if an initial diagnosis had not prescribed HRT then none of the other provisions would have automatically followed. In that particular case, permission was given by the Home Office to apply for surgery, but initially no funding was made available. The person's home health authority, after much wrangling, have said that they will both authorise and find the surgery and the outcome is awaited – most eagerly by the prisoner herself. Once surgery is complete, we understand that the prisoner will then serve the remainder of the sentence in a women's prison.

It must be acknowledged that that will not be the end of the story, and that other difficulties regarding status and integration are anticipated by professionals, but we understand the person herself is totally optimistic of her future.

There are difficulties also for outside workers in obtaining information about developments from prisons, and it is also difficult to provide an integrated level of support. The authors found that there are other practitioners within the probation service who have prisoners and offenders in the community but who do not have the time to form an information and support group, so each works in isolation and in potential ignorance. Equally, we assume there are prison staff grappling with the same issues and feelings whilst trying to manage inmates safely. The problems we experience in providing through care for transsexuals are an exacerbated version of problems inherent in the system. It would, however, be simplistic to assume that the answers lie solely in better co-ordination between the two services or better organised practitioner support groups. Transsexuals will not get a coherent service until the prejudice that surrounds them is de-mystified and challenged.

Transsexual Prisoners and Housing

When a prisoner is discharged into the community other issues arise. We found that the local authorities which we contacted were generally sympathetic. With regard to hostel provision on the other hand, the situation was less clear. It was obvious that no policies existed and that the issues had not been grasped. Rehabilitation and resettlement of offenders is always difficult. When the offender is a transperson there are additional dimensions to the difficulties. The local authorities contacted were willing to consider the application for accommodation pending the usual considerations about risk and dangerousness. But Local Authority Exclusion Policies may make this situation more difficult. There are also issues about the area in which the housing could be provided, and possible discrimination and prejudice from the community in which the person is to be resettled.

When we approached probation service hostels in our own area they had not encountered the questions previously but endeavoured to make a considered and thoughtful response. One provider had access to both a mixed and a special needs hostel. In the latter, additional support could be given but there remained a lot of further considerations. There was uncertainty about whether the transperson would go into a male or female hostel if only HRT had been prescribed, or whether the addition of gender reassignment surgery would make a difference to the designation. Clearly this raises a lot of discussion and providers said that, in addition to the usual factors of risk, appropriateness and so on, gender reassignment would be a factor. No provider refused. All acknowledged the issues we have outlined. We are aware that some housing associations, notably one in Manchester, are exploring the possibilities of housing projects with support for transpeople and we feel this is a positive move in the right direction.

If young people receive appropriate support, then they may be assisted to move on through the process of change positively. Sometimes, though, where medical treatment is inaccessible or expensive, young people may resort to prostitution in order to raise the necessary finance. As long as residential projects function on gender lines (and we believe this to be appropriate professionally for a range of reasons) transpeople will continue to raise issues for the system. Possibly separate provision may be one answer. However, there does need to be an informed recognition of acceptance of the needs of a transperson. It is also important that this awareness is underpinned by a positive legal framework of rights.

The Law and Employment

The law in Britain places a considerable number of restrictions on transsexuals. For example, marriage is unlawful. An originally recorded gender remains on all state records from birth to death. The adoption and fostering, together with access to children is effectively barred by statute and case law. Employment rights are also adversely affected. Detainment and imprisonment rights are not assured in the area of criminal law i.e. a female transperson, still a male on her birth certificate has no automatic right to detention as a female. The authors know of several transpeople confined within the male prison system who spend the bulk of their sentence in the hospital wing. Their use of clothing of choice, though allowed, is restricted. Regular contact with females on an equal basis is almost impossible. If they are battling to be acknowledged as transpeople and therefore need to receive counselling and apply for funding for treatment, there is the added stigma of being criminals serving a current sentence.

The rape of female transpeople is not chargeable as such and transpeople males and females are also open to prosecution for using the public toilets appointed for their new gender. The law as it stands leaves transpeople pre and post operatively in a minefield. Nevertheless, some changes are happening. In August, 1998 a male sergeant major who announced his plans to begin hormone replacement therapy and change his name was not to be dismissed from the Army. A spokesperson for the Ministry of Defence said: 'We have no policy on transsexuals other than that if a soldier is male or female they need to conform to standards of fitness like all other soldiers'. A medical examination would follow on which the soldier's future career would depend. An Army spokesperson also added that discrimination and bullying would not be tolerated. The soldier himself was pleased at how forward-thinking the Army had proved itself to be and hoped that it paved the way for other transsexuals in the Army. (The Guardian 6/8/1998).

A transperson's documentation, such as birth certificate, death certificate, driving licence and passport, all retain the original gender designation. Some examination boards have refused to re-issue certificates gained in the old name. City and Guilds, following objections, have now reviewed their policy and will change names. The authors have no information about other examination boards. This leaves transpeople open to repeated questioning, embarrassment and public humiliation.

These restrictions are being challenged by appeals to courts and the status of transpeople is being confirmed by new medical knowledge and the appointment of a professor of gender dysphoria in the Netherlands. This is the first appointment of its kind. In addition, following a consultation exercise with the Department of Education and some ferocious lobbying the Equal Opportunities Commission has produced proposals for legislation which would replace the Equal Pay Act and Sex Discrimination Act. It is proposed that gender reassignment would be included and that discrimination against transpeople would be illegal. If adopted such legislation would transform all areas of life.

Funding

It is important that practitioners have some understanding of the discussion and principles behind diagnosis, treatment and funding, which will dominate a transpersons life. In January, 1996 a report was produced by the Parliamentary Forum entitled *Transsexualism: The Current Medical Viewpoint*. The report discussed the issues in terms of transsexualism being a 'gender identity disorder', requiring diagnosis and treatment but does make out a strong case for legal recognition for transsexuals under the law saying that it is a matter of concern to the UK medical community that:

> *the current legal status of people who have been treated for transsexualism works against the achievement of these performance indicators, i.e. quality of life as defined by the right to employment, relationships, integration and fulfilment.* (Reid and Jones 1996)

O'Keefe and Fox challenge this view of transsexualism as a disorder. They comment that 'it fails to see sex and gender as a fluid continuum referring to opposite sexes in comparison with the bipolar reproductive model' but they do acknowledge, despite this, that the paper is a step in the right direction and may be useful for those involved in the fight for legal recognition and equality (O'Keefe and Fox, 1997).

In December, 1998 three transsexuals won their legal battle against North West Lancashire Health Authority's decision to refuse them treatment, on the basis it was unlawful. This landmark ruling at the Court of Appeal 'recognised the condition as a legitimate illness' (Mr Justice Hidden 21.12.98). There may remain a debate as to the terminology but that ruling will have implications for all health authorities in the future. On a more cautious note, we wonder if it will affect the length of time transsexuals have to wait for agreed treatment.

The Medical View

Despite the above mentioned support there are controversies about the funding of the surgery which is required. The Suffolk Health Authority view (Report, May, 1994) assesses the total cost of one person's treatment as around £50,000. Only about 10 per cent of those treated by surgery in the British overall review in 1984 thought that surgery had been a failure, (Suffolk H.A., 1994) The Suffolk report comes to the conclusion that 90 per cent of patients benefit from treatment, but also notes that lack of 'technical success' of surgery has an impact on the overall outcome.

As a guide to practitioners the following information may be of help in understanding how assessments for gender reassignment are made by psychiatrists.

Good Candidates

Life-long cross-gender identification.

Inability to adopt or live in assigned biological gender role.

Capacity to pass effortlessly and convincingly in society.

Not considered to gain sexual arousal from cross dressing.

Demonstration of stability, holding the same job for years, long-term relationships, etc.

First heterosexual experience, if any, was in adulthood rather than in early adolescence.

Some higher education.

Willingness to accept and actively participate in psychotherapy before and after surgery.

Presence of adequate social and family support.

Completion of a programme at a recognised gender identity clinic.

Living and working for at least two years as a member of the opposite sex.

At least one year of medically supervised hormone treatment.

Poor Candidates

Absence of characteristics of good candidate.

Active or recent thought disorder.

History of significant anti-social behaviour.

Exclusively uses cross-dressing for sexual arousal.

Recent major loss or emotional crisis.

Multiple suicide attempts including self mutilation of genitals.

Substance misuse.

Unrealistic expectations of surgery.

By-passing normal channels of care, such as obtaining hormones illicitly, or obtaining surgery elsewhere.

After a long term relationship, the psychotherapist resists referral for surgery.

After a long-term relationship, the
  psychotherapist feels relatively
  comfortable in referring the
  patient for surgery.
Absence of any characteristics of
  poor candidate.

(Chart from Suffolk Health Authority, May, 1994)

For probation officers and others trying to advise transpeople, it is particularly important to realise how anti-social and criminal behaviour features in both lists, linked with an unstable personality and factors indicating a poor likelihood of a successful outcome. It is also our experience that surgery is often seen as a solution to a whole range of difficulties and problems which may or may not be linked with gender dysphoria. From a probation perspective this point reminds us of the need already discussed to separate out offence focused issues from issues of gender dysphoria.

Funding is always going to be an obstacle with gender reassignment surgery. If the individual is an offender or serving prisoner there is likely to be additional reluctance to fund this process as it may be perceived that there are more 'deserving cases' for overstretched funding. Gender reassignment surgery is expensive and may be perceived by the public as a waste of resources.

Activists have expressed concerns about access to surgery and the quality delivered. The Nottingham Health Authority have a local policy which currently makes provision for two gender reassignment procedures per year, a policy which might provide a model for elsewhere (Practice Guidelines: Nottingham Health Authority, 1997).

Conclusion

In the last century, death, by which the Victorians were surrounded, was the great topic for discussion. At the end of the 20th century death is the great taboo subject, whilst discussion about sex seems an obsession. However, we would question how open and honest that debate has been. Analysis has traditionally been bipolar with male and female distinctly defined and each sex destined for copulation with the other. Power and authority has been given exclusively to males and within that grouping males who obeyed the rules of gendered behaviour. Homosexuality amongst women was considered not to exist, or if it did, to be a passing phase. For men, homosexuality was an illness, a weakness, a curse to be dreaded and fought.

The Christian church traditionally reinforced this male-orientated heterosexual definition of acceptable sexuality. It is interesting, then, that some Christians point to Old Testament quotations when validating heterosexuality, and appropriate gendered behaviour whilst ignoring many others relating to dietary laws and rules.

It could be said that there is an inherent anomaly that the teachings of a man who remained a confirmed bachelor, associated with twelve men apparently selected at random, and spent years in their company, should be considered a basis for heterosexual family life. Furthermore, his mother conceived him whilst unmarried. We offer this analogy to illustrate the social construct of prejudice. If this account of the church's belief is distorted, then we would say, so too is the distorted, narrow and oppressive definitions of sexuality which for so long have dominated debate. O'Keefe and Fox (1997) offer a list of up to twelve sexualities and there may be others which people may feel the need to add. It is not necessary to know the terms, but is necessary to understand and accept the diversity of sexuality as experienced by individuals.

Why cannot more sexualities be accepted and considered as enriching human life in all its variety and excitement? Why do so many people spend so much time in defining other people's sexuality negatively and making life miserable for those who fail to conform?

Again, O'Keefe and Fox ask, why was the concept of a third sex invented? They conclude that the 'the establishment was attempting to be free of all responsibility for what it conceived as the deviant behaviour of transsexuals' (O'Keefe and Fox, 1997). As professionals, we will all have engaged in discussions about deviancy at some time in our careers. Here we are again, faced with the word 'deviant'. Deviant from what norm we ask and whose purpose is this norm serving? As probation officers we can see that transsexuals who are offenders may harm themselves and others by their offending behaviour. It is difficult to see who they harm by being transsexual, the harm if there is such is done by the recipients own prejudices and those of others. Thus we ask why are transsexuals made to overcome so many obstacles and hurdles in achieving their goals? Official designation of gender at birth only allows for two choices, well intentioned decisions that are made relatively quickly but are legally enforceable for that person's life. Why are not the wishes of adult individuals paramount?

Would it be possible for society to develop a wider view of gender? If that was the case, perhaps such massively invasive (and expensive) surgery would be not needed as at present to define a person as either male or female. Equally in the context of our own work place, perhaps it would be easier to analyse risky and dangerous behaviour free from prejudicial assumptions and thus to really engage in public protection work.

This chapter has been designed to help practitioners raise awareness of the issues, to provide information, to get people to question their own assumptions, and to be sensitive to the issues of transpeople. We hope we have provided an informed framework, which can be applied to practice and which will help colleagues feel more comfortable in working with transpeople. The list of resources and contact points, together with further reading from the book list, will help colleagues who wish to know more.

References

Barter, S. (1997) Long Term Imprisonment, Men And Sex. *Probation Journal*. V:44: No. 1.

Bornstein, K. (1994) *Gender Outlaw*. NY and London: Routledge.

Burns, C. and McNab, C. (1996) and (1999) Press and Information Releases, London: Press For Change.

Cook-Deegan, R. (1994) *The Gene Wars. Science, Politics and the Human Genome*. USA: Norton.

Consultation Paper. *Legislation Regarding Discrimination On Grounds Of Transsexualism In Employment* (1998) London: Department of Education and Employment.

Gender Dysphoria Trust International. (1992) *The Reality*. London: GDTI.

Gentlement, A. (1998) Army Agrees Joe Can Be Joanne. *The Guardian* 6.8.98.

Hidden, Mr Justice. (1998) High Court Ruling. Quoted in *The Guardian. The Times*. 22.12.98.

Mcgrath, B.(1998) Sex-Change Ban Is Lifted. *Nottingham Evening Post*. 30.4.98.

Nottingham Health Authority (1997) Good Practice Guidelines for HAS.

O'Keefe, T. and Fox, K. (1997) *Trans-X-Ual, The Naked Difference*. London: Extraordinary People Press.

Peterson, M. *International Study Of Rights Of Transpeople In Prison*. Canada.

Raymond, J. (198O) *The Transsexual Empire*. London: The Women's Press.

Raynor, J. (1998) The Third Sex. *Observer Life* 1.3.98.

Rees, M. (1996) *Dear Sir or Madam*. London and NY: Cassell.

Reid, Dr R. and Jones, L.M.P. (1996) *Transsexualism: The Current Medical Viewpoint*. Second Edition. The Parliamentary Forum Report. London.

Suffolk Health Authority (1994) *Transsexuals And Sex Reassignment Surgery. An Internal Report*. Suffolk H.A.

Taylor, T. (1996) *The Prehistory of Sex*. London: Fourth Estate Ltd.

The International Bill Of Gender Rights. (1993) Second International Conference On Transgender Laws And Employment Policy. Houston, Texas.

The Local Government Management Board. (1998) Advisory Bulletin. Employment Relations No 375, London.

Groups and Organisations

The authors would like to thank Press for Change for their excellent web site; http://www.pfc.org.uk/

Postal Address: Press for Change, BM Network, London WCIN 3XX.

Press For Change are the true experts on this subject and should be contacted for up to date information. The web site offers full reading lists, a comprehensive list of printed information available by post, some free some for a small charge. We would highly recommend any interested party making contact with Press for Change.

The Gender Trust/The Beaumont Soc. http://www.gentrust.freeserve.co.uk. London, WC1N 3XX also publish an excellent handbook, and a book 'Transvestism, Transsexualism and the Law' by Melanie McMullan and Stephen Whittle can be obtained from them.

Mermaids. BM Mermaids London. WC1N3XX.

Support Group for families and friends of transsexual children and adolescents.

Vaginoplasty Network (South), c/o Ms. Hilary Everett, Gynaecology Social Worker, Social Services Dept., St Bartholomew's Hospital, West Smithfield, London EC1A 7BE.

Vaginoplasty Network (North), c/o Ms. Sheila Naish, Royd Well Counselling, 35 Royd Terrace, Hebden Bridge, West Yorks. HX7 7BT.

The Gender Identity Clinic, Charing Cross Hospital, London. Tel: 0181 846 1234.

Internet and World Web Sites

Transgender Forum (weekly E-zine) http://www.tgforum.com

Transgender Forum Resource Centre http://www.tgfmall.com

Transgender Forum Community Centre http://www.transgender.org/tg

CHAPTER 9

Teaching and Training for Change: Challenging Heterosexism

Jan Clare

Introduction

I am the co-ordinator for the Personal and Professional Development Module, which is the opening sequence on the Diploma in Social Work at the University of Central England, Birmingham. Although the teaching methods have undergone changes over the years, the learning in this module continues to provide a baseline from which all other learning develops. The aim of the teaching is for the students to understand the nature of power relationships through the oppression experienced by women, black people, older people, those with disabilities and those who are lesbian, gay or bisexual. Our belief, in the School of Social Work, is that we cannot understand and assess the needs of others without an understanding of how our own power, or lack of it, influences the way we see the world and the decisions we take. This sequence, more than any other, embodies explicitly the course philosophy. This requires of social work practitioners the ability to offer critical analysis of the various explanations of 'social reality', of behaviour and the ideologies that are often hidden in these explanations. Students, and staff, are helped to 'arrive at a better understanding of their own values, and to practise behaviours which give effective expression to the value base of the profession'.

In the probation service, where I spend the other half of my working life, the shared value base continues to preclude recruiting someone whose attitudes towards offenders are punitive. In spite of attempts by the last Conservative Home Secretary to modify the recruitment profile of probation trainees to include ex-armed service personnel, our present Home Secretary appears more concerned with reconviction rates than the type of person employed as probation staff. Thus the Personal and Professional Development module encourages students to examine their values and make the necessary adjustments in behaviour so that when they become social workers, they will be encouraged to provide a fair service based on an awareness of self. Whether future probation officers, presently being trained under the new arrangements, will have this shared perspective is uncertain. Anecdotal evidence suggests that any focus on understanding heterosexism is extremely remote!

When teaching on the sequence I draw on training I have delivered over many years. Particularly in relation to issues of sexuality, and more precisely on the oppression felt as a result of heterosexism, that is, the belief that heterosexual behaviour and relationships are the norm and that therefore other sexual relationships are abnormal and deviant. Most people will have never seriously considered the issue. As future social workers, if our students *have* considered the issue it will generally have been to confirm their liberal attitudes. They will have rarely considered it as another form of oppression or that their behaviour might contribute to the perpetuation of that oppression. After the first hour of teaching, students are recalling instances where they have encouraged homophobic jokes, made thoughtless or offensive comments to gay or lesbian friends and viewed the world entirely in relation to heterosexuality.

The first challenge to those beliefs is their surprise that a university lecturer should be 'brave enough' to be open about their sexuality. If it was as 'cool to be gay' as many believe, what makes it 'brave' to be 'out'? The students' personal response to me reflects this dichotomy. Some adopt a 'so what?' approach, others are overwhelmingly friendly. Generally, those that have a problem with the issue tend to steer clear of me, as do those students who wish to stay in the closet for fear that others might notice them talking to me and draw unwelcome conclusions. For 'out' students the response varies, obvious relief from some, of course, and a sad comment on one occasion from a student who wished the family who had disowned him could see that 'respectable' people like university lecturers could also be gay.

Students arrive on a social work course with the desire to help others and a belief that they can do so. Their life experiences have produced individuals who empathise with the distress of others and have an embryonic sense that somehow much of this distress is not accidental. Many will have been victims or survivors of oppression themselves; the last thing they want to do is victimise others. They arrive at an understanding fairly quickly however that dealing with any form of oppression requires more than good intentions and that their belief system, that hitherto had felt reasonably secure, was being challenged. They realise the difference between intention and effect; that kind, well-meaning people frequently deny rights to others.

Perhaps it is not altogether surprising that the routine oppression of lesbian, gay and bisexual people comes as a shock to most people. Long before the arrival of New Labour there were a number of prominent gay icons, both black and white. Generally in the sphere of entertainment, their very visibility led the general public to believe that, whilst being gay was still perhaps not completely acceptable, it was no longer something people felt they had to hide. There are gay cabinet ministers, an out, Asian member of the House of Lords, gay (and lesbian) MPs, television stars. Far from concealing their different sexuality, gay people looked as if they were having more fun, they didn't look oppressed. The increased visibility of lesbian and gay people has lead to the belief that things must be 'OK' or they would stay in the closet. Since they are not in the closet, and these public figures come to be seen as the *only* gay people around, there can't be a problem. And since they are now 'out' and therefore 'OK', it is acceptable to crack jokes about them and not be seen as offensive. I have lost count of the number of times George Michael has been called 'The Queen of Soul' on pop radio stations. The fact that 'out' public figures are wealthy conceals the way in which oppression operates. Lesbian and gay life experience is measured against these false norms. Black students know that the popularity of Frank Bruno, Imran Khan or Shefali, the weather 'girl', don't diminish either the structural or indeed individual oppression which is their daily experience.

Working with Sexuality

Teaching and training to raise awareness of any kind of oppression arouses fear and resistance. Few of us would intentionally wish to harm others but the understanding that has been developed in relation to racism in particular has demonstrated that good intentions alone rarely lead to justice. Thus, defensive attitudes are likely if our awareness is to be raised, someone is going to be challenging attitudes and behaviour that hitherto had served us well enough. Our sexuality is also something that involves many of our deepest experiences and whilst 'our' culture, and by that I mean dominant white culture, appears obsessed with sexual activity, few of us are able to communicate in a genuine way about what sex means to us.

Information is the obvious place to begin, information that demonstrates why being anything other than heterosexual is problematic. It comes as a surprise that there is no protective legislation for gay people comparable to the Sex or Race Discrimination Acts; or that the law is enthusiastically used on occasions to *prosecute* gay sexuality. There is astonishment about the attitudes of the judiciary in the family courts leading to lesbian mothers losing the right to bring up their children or gay fathers their right to access. It causes dismay that there is an absence of rights in relation to next of kin so that, among other things, lesbian and gay partners of long standing can be refused access to their loved ones in hospital. Even the right to attend their partner's funeral. The differential practices in relation to immigration (recently somewhat liberalised to bring the UK in line with Europe) is something generally only considered in relation to race and racism, not in relation to the forcible separation of lesbian and gay couples. The extent of the information, and I have only touched on a very small number of relevant issues here, and the fact that very little of this was known to students, helps remove defensive barriers and encourages the examination of attitudes they had believed were non-oppressive. They begin to examine some of the responses they have made in the past to friends who have come 'out' – 'what's the problem?' and ways in which they have begun to socialise their own children into heterosexuality. Here the learning frequently incorporates ideas about sexism and the rigid sex-role socialisation that induces parents to control and 'patrol' behaviour for fear of producing queer children. They begin to see that so much of what they had taken as acceptable about their attitudes, beliefs and behaviour amounts to oppression. There is often sadness at these discoveries, particularly about the hurt done to others and possibly to their own children.

How to Begin

I became a trainer before I was a teacher. What I was pleased to discover when I was sent on a Certificate in Education course was that attention to process is crucial if effective learning is to take place and that good teaching methods are very similar to good training techniques. I therefore try to unite the two in any learning activity. Thus, how the session begins is crucial. In dealing with issues of oppression we need to feel a degree of safety in order to learn. If we are afraid of censure or discovery we block our own learning.

In the Personal and Professional Development sequence there are two days of introduction during which the students and staff attempt to reach not only a shared intellectual understanding of oppression but some notion of how best that learning can take place and how that will need to affect behaviour. Sometimes this is more successful than others, sometimes students simply mouth what they think we want to hear rather than genuinely engage in a process of unlearning.

Since knowledge is power, or at least potentially empowering, information giving at the outset is often helpful in my experience. It gives participants the opportunity to listen and be alone with their thoughts before taking any risks themselves. It also provides a further opportunity to make judgements about the speaker and the amount of risk it is safe to take. Delivering a lecture is acceptable in a university, whereas training demands methods of interaction. In training workshops I generally begin by asking participants to write down what they *know* about lesbian and gay people. Two issues predominate. The first is that what they had believed was knowledge, is based on gross stereotypes. These range from the relatively harmless 'gay men are sensitive, lesbians are ugly' to the pernicious notions that any sexuality which is not heterosexual is perverted and harmful to others, particularly to children. The other is the lack of 'knowledge' about lesbian women.

All forms of oppression are underpinned by stereotypes; the surprise for our students is that *they* are doing the stereotyping. The issue of lesbian invisibility is rarely considered, even by those consciously trying not to discriminate. This is perhaps not surprising; there is no lesbian equivalent of Julian Clary or Boy George, no lesbian woman in the world of entertainment who is a popular figure or household name. Some may have heard of Sandi Toxvig or Sarah Bernhardt but they are hardly household names. Stereotyping also means that if you don't fit the notion of what a lesbian looks like, i.e. overweight, youthful, white, man-hating, nobody gives your sexuality a thought. This is reinforced by the sexual objectification of lesbian women by heterosexual men (much pornography contains reference to lesbianism, with the macho stud joining and dominating lesbians having sex) so that all 'ordinary' women who are neither sex-obsessed nor wielding whips are assumed to be heterosexual!

These awareness-raising exercises generally take place in separate racial groups. Before I joined the staff, teaching in this area was delivered by heterosexual staff, black and white, to mixed groups of students. Problems arose almost immediately; some black students raised concerns in relation to the conflict caused by their religious beliefs. Other black students would then challenge these comments and an argument would develop which the white students would passively observe. This resulted in white students developing the belief that homophobia was a problem for black people and that they themselves had little work to do. Tensions within the black group meant that the issue began to slide out of focus, because listening then stopped, personal needs were no longer being met and the old arguments about hierarchy of oppressions ensued. Lesbian, gay and bisexual students would be offended and distressed and the learning was disrupted for everyone. The dynamic of the whole student cohort was also damaged in the process.

Working in separate racial groups means that black students can share and explore their differing views in relative safety. A helpful exercise developed by a black colleague consists of asking the group to split up into factions that represent competing interests within a community. All views are heard and learning extended through the interchange that takes place. Through genuine listening the issues can be debated and when listening takes place people are able to shift their attitudes. The ability of the group to manage these differences adds to the cohesion of the group. If strong differences can be accommodated, confidence grows and the dynamic improves. Black students also need to be spared the stereotypes held by white people about black sexuality and in general welcome the space and privacy accorded to them on this and other occasions on the course.

The ability of tutors, both to support and challenge heterosexual students, is crucial and the same trust that black staff give to white staff when tackling racism is needed. Black staff in our department are strongly committed to anti-oppressive practice. They approach the issues with black students in ways that balance respect for religious conviction with challenge to behaviour that harms others. They require students to transfer knowledge of their own oppression to the treatment of lesbian and gay people. The confidence with which staff handle this provides helpful modelling, pointers for behavioural change and constructive challenge. The white group, without black students to carry out the debate for them, are obliged to address their own attitudes. These are frequently different only in the manner in which they are expressed or indeed *not* expressed. The same silence by white students that accompanies teaching on racism is one of the barriers to overcome when addressing homophobia and heterosexism.

Useful Material

The students are provided with a wide range of material which is aimed to promote their understanding and which integrates personal with professional concerns. Handouts such as the amusing quiz in the New Internationalist, *Do You Need Treatment?* which asks of heterosexuals the kinds of questions that are routinely put to lesbian and gay people: 'What do you think is the cause of your heterosexuality? 'Are you afraid of members of your own sex?' 'Don't you think your heterosexuality might be a phase you're going through?' etc. Using material that makes people laugh as well as learn is always helpful and contributes to a safe, relaxed atmosphere. It is also important to relate heterosexism to other forms of oppression. The article *'Fighting Racism and Homophobia – a United Battle'* that appeared in 'The Voice' from 'Black Lesbians and Gays Against Media Homophobia' following the late Justin Fashanu's coming out in 1990, is invariably provided. Information about the differential effects of ageism and disability on lesbian and gay people is disseminated. It is helpful if the material includes ideas around improved social work practice, such as the National Association of Probation Officers' policy document *'Working with Lesbians and Gay Men as Clients of the Service – Good Practice Guidelines'*. As our clear message is that the personal influences the professional, it is necessary that good information to challenge personal attitudes is used.

I believe that using different methods to deliver the same messages reinforces learning. Thus the use of games is integral to many of my teaching/training plans.

The Telepath Game

This is an exercise that can be used particularly effectively when participants are 'blocking' and failing to engage meaningfully with the oppression experienced by lesbian and gay people. It is also very helpful in relation to learning about other areas of oppression. I often use it when groups are denying that anything they do oppresses gay people and they are failing to see how their socialisation has influenced their attitudes and beliefs; 'some of my best friends are . . .' It is best carried out in groups of no more than twelve people but they must have no visible differences. All participants are given cards that identify them as either 'telepaths' or non-telepaths'. No one knows who is a telepath and who is not. The telepaths are advised on their cards that being telepathic is not generally acceptable, but that they can choose whether or not to disclose. They are told that they are isolated and need to contact other telepaths but need to be aware of their own safety.

The non-telepaths on the other hand are advised that they are frightened of telepaths. They have been told that most people are not telepathic and those that are, are easily recognisable. They are further advised that telepaths have no power to harm non-telepaths, but that if they meet a telepath they will try to make them telepathic. The full group is then left to devise three rules for this hypothetical society.

The learning from this game is richly rewarding as the telepaths struggle to make contact to lessen their isolation. They attempt to suss out who can be trusted and who cannot, but are inhibited from finding out the information that they need through fears for their own safety. The non-telepaths at the same time attempt to enforce rules that limit the liberty of telepaths, although some brave souls, mindful that telepaths cannot actually hurt them, speak up to protest at their treatment. They are generally, however, in a very small minority.

Thus the game, used to explore and understand heterosexism, exposes both blatant and subtle homophobia and raises questions, and provides answers, about the nature of collusive oppression and its effects upon us all. It exposes the harmful internalised self-beliefs which gay people develop and demonstrates starkly how stereotypes about gay people lead to oppressive assumptions and behaviour. The point the game perhaps makes best, and which makes it particularly meaningful in relation to heterosexism, are the risks involved in everyday transactions between gay and heterosexual people and that 'coming out' is potentially dangerous as well as something that requires hundreds of daily decisions. In fact this game is so full of learning that I have been tempted to substitute it for any other activities on training workshops because it illustrates both issues of content as well as process. Consider how we have as a 'rule' 'Everyone is equal' but this can be seen to be manifestly not so in a society where Acts of Parliament prevent such equality in relation to lesbian and gay people. The game also exposes how we can allow ourselves to believe that we are doing right simply by wishing it or saying the right things.

Some of the learning is directly transferable to other areas of oppression, particularly racism, where stereotyping influences attitudes and behaviour profoundly. What must be guarded against is losing the *point* of the game itself. Participants learn a lot about themselves and can find this more interesting than focusing on heterosexism. The role of the facilitator is to ensure that the necessary connections are made.

Supporting Lesbian and Gay Students

I always invite lesbian/gay and bisexual students to spend part of the day working with me. This invitation serves a number of purposes. It allows lesbian, gay and bisexual students to meet together for the first time. It is important for this to happen, as there is sometimes limited understanding and awareness of the other lesbian and gay students on the course. Also, the beginning of the course is a time of anxiety for all students. The knowledge that there are others like you, even though we all know there must be, is a relief and there are lots of exchanges along the lines of 'I thought maybe you were, but then you talked about your four kids ...' etc. It also provides an opportunity for them to have access to an out lesbian manager/lecturer and perhaps express some of the fears all students are experiencing at that point. More importantly, it provides a safe place where these students can be supported and understood, without having to explain in great detail what they mean and without fear of being on the receiving end of heterosexist ignorance, prejudice or patronage. That same space is provided for other groups when we deal with related areas of oppression and is often initially resisted. It is only when students feel the benefits of a strong group identity that they begin to see the point.

The decision to accept my invitation is not an easy one for those students that do. Most of them have, until then, concealed their sexuality from their peers. There is no pressure placed upon them and I raise related issues in the lecture beforehand so that heterosexual students have an understanding of what the decision entails. It is this group who need to realise the risks involved in coming out and that once it's done there is no going back. They will never see those students in the same way as they once did and they will already have become conscious of false assumptions they have made and possible offence caused. Heterosexual students also need to appreciate that for the 'out' students this is yet another coming out and that the consideration of whether to be 'out' or not is made a hundred times every day. That this particular day's experience may stimulate other, perhaps difficult, memories of other 'outings', other hurts. From the lecture, students will know some of the risks that those who are parents face when they are known to be gay. They should also understand some of the reasons why black lesbian and gay people will choose to face racism rather than look at the issues around their own sexuality. That they may have to face a choice of concealment of their sexuality, rather than lose the support of other black students in challenging racism.

There will always be a proportion of students who are neither willing nor able to come out and 'choose' to join the other groups. Sometimes they tell me that this is what they are going to do, sometimes they don't. I am fairly certain that some of them will never be confident enough to reveal their sexuality and will suffer as a consequence. The best I can do is to encourage and support where I can, but even this can be threatening to someone who is desperate to conceal his or her sexuality. The hard truth is that in spite of an 'out' lesbian lecturer, a committed and racially mixed staff group and the school's culture and history of anti-discriminatory practice, it stills feels unsafe to be 'out' for some. From time to time I experience a sense of panic and remember frightening instances of exposure in my own life. The anxiety never quite goes away that they will be repeated in spite of my privileged position and the 'protection' (I do experience it that way) of being 'out' in all areas of my professional life. If I feel such fear, how must students feel? At times I question whether or not I should be involved in the teaching. Maybe it should remain the responsibility of colleagues in the department. Since I teach on all other forms of oppression in the sequence it does not make sense to avoid teaching on the area I know best. I feel it is important to model to all students that 'out' gay people can be in positions of power, and survive.

More recently I have invited a local gay team manager, who is white, to share both the lecture input with me and the subsequent support group for the students. It feels important that there is a gay male presence as well as someone who can speak authoritatively on the everyday reality of being an 'out' gay practitioner. It is also enjoyable for me to exchange views with a gay professional with a different approach from mine. He has developed my thinking by challenging from a supportive position. I wish there were other lesbian or gay staff who could share the responsibility of the teaching with me and with whom I could check out my uncertainties, but there aren't, and that is the reality for lesbian women or gay men in most other areas of life.

The (generally small) group of students that spends the day with us often feels split between wanting to hear and challenge the views of heterosexual students and at the same time thankful to relax with supportive others. They are conscious that both the facilitators are white and therefore limited in what we can offer to students who are not, but until the work is recognised and there are other black staff members this situation will continue to reflect the dilemma.

My relationship with these lesbian and gay students is different from the one I have with heterosexual students. I am still regarded as a lecturer and therefore powerful (and thus potentially oppressive) but I am also someone whose life experience contains major similarities. These include the discovery of a different sexuality from others around us, feelings of isolation and fear, being rejected by people important to us, coming and/or being 'out', the struggle to maintain a balanced, functioning approach to life, etc. The time spent with them becomes more one of support than of learning and the difference in power between us becomes less significant. Past students have commented upon the importance of having a visible gay presence, and its relevance to their learning should not be underestimated. Again, parallels can be drawn with other groups of students who experience other forms of structural disadvantage. Learning, not only support, should occur however, and this needs to focus on helping those students deal with the consequences of the oppression they experience and finding and maintaining positive coping strategies.

Evaluating Teaching and Training

Evaluating any teaching or training is a tricky business: written feedback forms, or 'happy sheets', as they are sometimes irreverently called, only provide limited information. I discovered long ago that simply enjoying something means nothing more than that, and that once the immediate emotional impact of a piece of teaching or training has receded, all that is left is a memory of the event. How do we ever know that experiential learning such as this has had an impact that goes beyond feeling and thought to action and changed practice? My own evidence is patchy and unscientific – I have experienced students challenging their own and others' behaviour and witnessed the shameful recalling of previously held attitudes. I am unable to claim more than that, but I have become convinced that any learning in areas such as these needs to be both challenging and supportive if it is to have any chance of success. If, as teachers and trainers, we start from the belief that human beings can change, and as a probation officer I hold firmly to this notion, we are constantly rewarded by the commitment of others. If the teaching is based on real respect for all our differences then we move forward together, rather than competing for our differing needs to be met.

Taking risks, I believe, invariably pays off. If students can see that a middle-aged white lecturer can be open about her sexuality and is supported by all other staff in word and deed, stereotypes are shattered and ways of behaviour modelled that can be imitated to promote change. This requires some courage but far less than we fear in our imagination. I remember a journalist from a local newspaper visiting the campus and attempting to suggest that he had heard a student was having a gay relationship with one of the lecturers. Of course, the assumption was that the lecturer was male! The students sent him on his way and then warned us of what they had done. We never heard from the journalist again. This has echoes of other similar occurrences that all lesbian and gay people will have experienced – it's part of the context – but dealing with them openly and refusing to be on the defensive is often all that is necessary.

My overall experience of teaching and training in relation to heterosexism has been positive; people will sometimes make insensitive or ill informed comments but the degree of resistance to the learning is far less than responses I have experienced from white people confronted with their racism. I think that might be something to do with the depth of shame and guilt white people feel towards black people and the defensiveness about being exposed as racist. Few but the rabid minority feel any degree of ease at accepting their own racism; the rest of us are on a continuum between complete denial and sorrowful acknowledgement. Lesbian and gay people have no collective history, no real, or not much, experience of 'community' and the shared psychic guilt of others does not exist. In my experience people seem almost relieved to shed their homophobia and make sense of their previous attitudes once they have the information and opportunity to do so. Belief systems are challenged, attitudinal shifts are made, and small but significant adjustments to behaviour take place, but this feels like a realistic starting point. We only have to look at our own individual ability and willingness to change to appreciate the difficulties others experience.

References

Brown, H.C. (1992) Lesbians, The State and Social Work Practice, in Langan, M. and Day, L. (Eds), *Women, Oppression and Social Work*. London: Routledge.

Brown, H.C. (1998) *Social Work and Sexuality: Working With Lesbians and Gay Men*. London: Macmillan.

Davies, D. and Neal, C. (1996) *Pink Therapy: A Guide for Counsellors and Therapists Working with Lesbian, Gay and Bisexual Clients*. Buckingham: Open University Press.

Lorde, A. (1982) *Zami: A New Spelling of my Name*. London: Sheba.

Logan, J., Kershaw, S., Karban, K., Mitts, S., Trotter, J. and Sinclair, M. (1996) *Confronting Prejudice: Lesbian and Gay Issues in Social Work Education*. Aldershot: Arena.

Mason-John, V. (Ed.) (1995) *Talking Black: Lesbians of African and Asian Descent Speak Out*. London: Cassell.

National Association of Probation Officers (1989) *Working with Lesbian and Gay Men as Clients of the Service: Good Practice Guidelines*. London: NAPO.

New Internationalist (November, 1989) *Pride and Prejudice: Homosexuality*.

The Voice (1991) *Fighting Racism and Homophobia – a United Battle*. 29 October, 1991.

Weeks, J. (1995) *Invented Moralities: Sexual Values in an Age of Uncertainty*. Cambridge: Polity Press.

Young People Now (1992) *Culture Clash*. 20 March, 1992.

Conclusion

Karen Buckley and Paul Head

In setting up this particular collection of essays we have tried to do a number of things.

First and foremost we have tried to establish logical connections between a collection of themes around oppression and stereotyping. We have done this because we believe that it is their very separation which allows them to elude deconstruction. Our message is that processes based on such thinking are dangerous and inherently flawed. They lead to false security and a failure to judge risk correctly.

Secondly we have tried to present the views and experiences of practitioners, those whose daily work brings them into contact with the damage that such forces bring. Such voices are often not heard. It is assumed that people practice on safe ground, according to established rules. Practice is not like that however. It often starts where the text book leaves off as the chapter on working with transgender people illustrates amply. Likewise it requires the integration of established thought with new ideas and an openness to the experience of minorities. It has been a long hard struggle for black or gay or feminist groups to get their issues taken seriously for example and it is arguable that they are not yet informing mainstream practice in more than a piecemeal fashion.

Practice is also where policies and ideas are road tested for their implications. Maggie Metcalfe, for example, has documented her concerns about risk assessment formulas as they apply to women and evidenced their limitations in practice. Michelle Meloy has had substantial experience of working as a probation officer in the USA where community notification procedures are far more advanced and formalised than in England. She points to the fallacies inherent in assuming that laws can make a community safer.

We would argue that the main thrust of integration of ideas is not, as may have been thought, about simple empowerment or rights. This is, in a sense, though worthy, a means to an end. That end is about a safer society where effective analysis of what constitutes dangerous behaviour happens as a result of clear, and not prejudice ridden, thought.

In Practice

Such practice is often working on the edge of the known, and it can be stressful to the worker. Learning experiences are personally challenging, as Ted Perry's chapter illustrates. Many of our authors have had the experience of being seen as eccentrics or enthusiasts in a way that seeks to devalue the message by devaluing the messenger. Frequently it takes a long time for an agency support structures to catch up with the needs of individual workers as the whole history of risk management indicates (see Buckley and Perry, 1993). Sometimes, as Jo Thompson and Victoria Hodgett illustrate, there seems a lack of will to do this. As Maggie Metcalfe indicates, identifying dangerousness in women has long been hampered by seeing them as substitute men or by trying to use the same proformas and tools for analysis.

So finally we have tried to establish the centrality of stereotypical thinking to the failures of social work practice in its broadest sense to tackle issues of risk and dangerousness. This for us, as editors, has been the ultimate goal.

Social work has often been accused in the past of naiveté or of over identification with the views and needs of its customers, and likewise an espousal of an equalities perspective has been seen as just pandering to political correctness. We hope that some of the work in this book has begun to illustrate that it is only when the world is viewed clearly and holistically that the damage that human beings do to each other can be assessed.

To obtain such a clear view one has to deconstruct much learned behaviour and attitudes of one's own, as well as on the part of the society we live in. Two of the chapters particularly, those by Clarence Allen and Jan Clare, offer examples of how to offer training in this context. The chapters by Ted Perry and Maggie Metcalfe offer some insight into the personal journeys that may be taken.

When we are interviewing or simply meeting people, how we deal with them is affected, whether we know it or not, by our instinctive likes or dislikes and social work professionals are not always any more sophisticated in this process than anyone else. We would suggest that some of this liking may have to do with sexuality, and the possibility that are we drawn to these people. They may impress us as attractive.

We may also be drawn to people because we experience them as powerful, personally and sexually, and want to be validated by them, or protected by this power. Many of the unheeded efforts of women around men can be deconstructed in this way, for example, and one can debate for hours as to whether the victims of sexism should be blamed for trying to make use of the system as they find it. Ultimately, until we deconstruct and recognise the process we will not in any event start to change the position of victims or make it easier for them to behave differently.

Our concern is that unless we recognise this process, for what it is, it will hamper our judgement, perhaps the more attractive will be valued, or more importantly, perhaps we will not see the danger correctly.

In effect, no matter how 'professional' we like to view ourselves as, elements of this sexual and social transference affect our behaviours. Ignoring this responsivity leads to denial of our influence and impact. It also leads to covert oppression, as people who will not or cannot be colonised in to the game have to be managed, or taught a lesson. Gender is a classification system backed up by patriarchy and the family.

We sometimes fail to consider power in the context of analysing human relationships. Our society was founded on patriarchy and remains based on the unequal and exclusive concept of the family. The family in its turn requires a strict system of gender classification to survive. It also has rules of engagement which may be societally specific.

From the perspective of these chapters it appears to be normalised, so that we do not readily analyse it, hence the failure to acknowledge that more child abuse takes place within the family than outside it. Features of society which lie outside its boundaries are suspect, the extended, or alternative family being one example. Equally the single parent headed family, often now the norm, is viewed with suspicion.

Where Next?

We are aware that there are many areas of work that we haven't touched on, that these factors impinge on, and we would like to stimulate debate as well as further work. Networking amongst practitioners needs to go on constantly and to be stimulated by training activity and budgets.

We are conscious, if not proud, that this is an account of practice, written largely by practitioners, and of experience written by the experienced. We hope that the thinking will open up debate which will lead to more evaluative research.

The next question that any editors have to set themselves is 'where next? What do we make of what we have found?'

The first issue is clearly about the need for integration. We are not arguing for the abandonment of single issue campaigns. They are effective in getting matters on the table and issues addressed at least in a piecemeal fashion. The refuge movement for example with its emphasis on violence as a function of male/female power relations may have seemed to marginalise male on male violence or black issues but it has also fairly and squarely paved the way for legal and political attention to relationship violence in a serious manner.

Equally, when planning a single issue venture it is important that implications for other groups are considered. Clarence Allen's chapter illustrates some of his experiences as a black gay male trainer often finding courses wanting on this basis: avoiding his experience in relation either to his blackness or his gay identity. One might wish to enlighten consciousness in one area, but find other discriminatory attitudes get in the way as Jan Clare's account describes when white students seek to distance themselves from homophobia by dumping it on black ones.

However, it seems important that somehow an integration begins to happen, an overall plan is developed that acts as an umbrella and where these things fit together. Perhaps this has to be done on some kind of agency or topic basis.

As editors we both work within the criminal justice sector, and the link we can thus perhaps see most clearly is the assessment of risk, because that is the central plank of our work. To take the example of gay men, as long as they are seen as entirely sexual they will always be seen as risky and their victimhood will always be subordinated to their perceived risk to heterosexuals.

This risk we need to remember is not just about sexuality but about challenge to established ways of living. If the current system of heterosexual stereotyping works so well, why can't it take a little challenge. Perhaps we need to honestly examine the nature of family structures and the damage we do before we subscribe to the philosophy that they are 'the best way'. Likewise, as long as black people are viewed as in any way more dangerous or criminal, any risks will be over-emphasised.

The next thing that occurs to us is a need for training. Jan Clare's chapter offers some suggestions on how to do this. Many of the authors in this work have informed themselves either by personal experience or by going outside their organisations. What we hope to demonstrate is that practice can develop itself, but that needs resourcing. Putting cross agency groups together with facilitation is not expensive except in terms of time but it argues for a different style of training than bringing in experts to tell all. The knowledge base may be within all of us if we are freed up.

Another strand to the debate is the question of hearing the message. Listening to challenge produces a healthier society.

Equally, we need to listen to the support and supervision needs of those who do this work. Whether it is in challenging abusive behaviour, or supporting redefinition of and affirmation of positive identity the worker is treading on ground which leads both to personal introspection of a painful sort and also the shared pain of victims. Unfortunately, as many chapters point out, organisational structures are often well behind their workers in this respect.

Conclusion

This book has essentially been about practitioners writing. We wanted to do this because we were aware of the skilful work our colleagues were undertaking, of the ground that they were breaking, and we wanted to share this. This is not a collection of research documents, nor is it necessarily the final word on many topics.

We think that it can point researchers in some directions however. It is time, for example, for a real look at same-sex violence that consults with victims. It is time also for an open look at the rights and needs of transgender people. Leonie Williams and David Phillips outline amply what needs doing but again perhaps it is transgender people who need consulting and not medicalising. It is, finally, time for a very critical look at stereotypical family structures so advocated as the right way by successive governments.

One of the difficulties we face is that compartmentalisation is simple, it makes life easy. If you can divide the world into two genders, ascribe behaviour to each, you can manage them, albeit as Maggie Metcalfe points out, sometimes to the marginalistion of one group.

Likewise, if you can stigmatise black people and suggest they are all the same it allows for comfortable thinking. What you do not have to contemplate is the immense variety of human behaviour, you do not need judgement, or sophisticated instruments for managing human behaviour. Anyone can do it. This is not to say that clinical judgement does not need tools, but that it needs to be valued for what it is, judgement which is only as good as the parameters on which it is based.

Finally, we would like to thank our contributors for their work and their courage. They have variously been able to quote their source material, but they are largely talking of their experience and the development of their own thinking and sometimes of the mistakes they have made. It is an exposed position, more difficult than writing up a piece of research and we commend them. Michelle Meloy's chapter ends with the personal observation that she wishes 'someone' would ask questions. We hope that collectively we have all posed some.

Reference

Buckley, K. and Perry, E. (1993) Supervision, Staff and Sexually Violent Offenders *NAPO News*. Sept. pp8–9.

Index

Index